305. 56

BELOW THE BREADLINE

Fran Abrams is an investigative journalist who spent more than ten
years on the staff of various national broadsheet newspapers, including
the *Independent*, the *Sunday Telegraph* and the *Sunday Times*. Her
freelance work has included assignments for the Guardian and BBC
Radio 4. Originally from Stockport, Greater Manchester, she lives in
Suffolk. She is currently writing

D0271243

FRAN ABRAMS

BELOW THE BREADLINE

LIVING ON THE MINIMUM WAGE

PROFILE BOOKS

First published in Great Britain in 2002 by
Profile Books Ltd
58A Hatton Garden
London ECIN 8LX
www.profilebooks.co.uk

Copyright © Fran Abrams, 2002

10 9 8 7 6 5 4 3 2

Typeset in Minion by MacGuru
info@macguru.org.uk

Printed and bound in Great Britain by
Bookmarque Ltd, Croydon, Surrey

The moral right of the author has been asserted.

A CIP catalogue record for this book is available from the
British Library.

ISBN 1 86197 471 X

CONTENTS

INTRODUCTION

Let me tell you about the nearly poor. They are, to misquote F. Scott Fitzgerald, different from you and me. They are soft where we are hard, cynical where we are trustful, in a way that, unless you were born poor, it is very difficult to understand. They think, deep in their hearts, that they are less than we are. Even when they enter far into our world, they still think they are less than we are. They are different.

This is not a book about defiant, angry people. This is not a book about the torrid cauldron of social unrest, where unseen passions sizzle and ferment under a boiling surface. This is a book about keeping your head down. Making the best of it. Making do with what you think you deserve. If people were houses, the characters in this book would be parked on some 1960s outer-ring estate, ignored and forgotten. They lack the grubby, inner-city allure of those at the very bottom of the heap. The homeless. The addicts. The refugees. And so, when the spoils of the latest anti-poverty measure are passed around, they probably aren't even there. They're at work, or standing at a bus stop somewhere with their shopping bags. Thinking it isn't about them.

Perhaps this does not sound very alluring. Perhaps these often marginalised people do not appear at first glance to have a great deal of interest about them. But even dingy semis on outer-ring estates can have sunflowers growing in their gardens. They can, if it is the season for it, be ablaze with Christmas lights. They can have outrageous scarlet-painted doors and windows or multi-coloured stone cladding. Just because you've got the imprint of someone else's boot on your forehead, it doesn't mean you're boring. It doesn't mean you never have any fun. You just have to work harder at it, that's all.

*

The chain of events that led to this book being written started with a Friday afternoon phone call in July 2001 from Ian Katz, the G2 editor of the *Guardian* newspaper. He had recently returned from the US, where he had heard about Barbara Ehrenreich's book *Nickel and Dimed*, an account of living on low pay in America. This had led him to wonder what life would be like on the minimum wage in London, indeed, whether it would be possible at all to live in England's capital on the national minimum, which had been introduced two years earlier at £3.60 per hour and later increased to £3.70. How would I like to find out?

We agreed that I would try to live on the minimum for a month, taking whatever work and accommodation I could get. My initial research, though, suggested there might not be much of a story. Figures from the Low Pay Unit suggested that only a tiny proportion of workers in London, probably less than 2 per cent, were earning the minimum wage. I began to wonder whether I would find all the available jobs paid far more than £3.70 an hour. These fears turned out to be ill-founded, though. On my first visit to the job centre there were about a dozen jobs advertised at or around the minimum, including posts for cleaners, supermarket checkout assistants and gardeners, though I had to rule out the latter because it required applicants to have both experience and a car. After all, even 2 per cent of workers adds up to a total of around 60,000 people earning the minimum wage in London.

I looked for a job which would allow me to work forty hours a week, taking my pre-tax pay to £148 per week, or just under £7,700 a year. After tax and national insurance, my rough calculations suggested I should take home around £130 per week. From that, I would need to spend at least £10 a week on transport and maybe £60 on accommodation in a shared house or bedsit. On the face of it it seemed possible that I would be able to survive, even though the average worker in London earns £560 per week

– almost four times the minimum. I certainly wouldn't be able to socialise in any of the capital's pubs, where a pint of lager cost around £2, but it seemed I would be able to eat.

The reality turned out to be much more grim. But this was London, one of the most expensive cities in the world. What about other parts of the UK? What would life be like on the minimum wage there? Would the people on low wages in the provinces be from marginalised groups, mostly recent immigrants, as they were in London? Or would they be from settled indigenous communities where the support systems were stronger and the cost of living lower? I set out to spend two more months living and working on the minimum wage, the first in Yorkshire and the second in Scotland.

Although the project started out being purely about life on the minimum wage, it grew in scope as it metamorphosed from a series of newspaper articles into a book. It seemed to me that the pensioner I met living in a boarded-up room, the elderly people with dementia I saw bullied and left to sit in their own urine by workers who were supposed to be caring for them, deserved to be mentioned. They were, after all, part of the tapestry of life on the breadline as I saw it. Like many of the low-paid workers I met, they were living at a junction where the 'respectable' world meets the underclass.

When the minimum wage was introduced in March

1999, the Chairman of the Low Pay Commission, George Bain, said its members had been struck by a comment made on a visit to Northern Ireland, and echoed elsewhere, that the low-paid were often on 'the margins of degradation'. He hoped the new minimum rate would allow them to play a fuller role in Britain's economic and social life: 'The introduction of a statutory floor for wage levels must encourage feelings of belonging not to the margins, but to the mainstream of society.'

I met many of those people on my travels, and witnessed their often valiant attempts to do as Professor Bain urged – to swim in the middle of the stream, to live the same lives, maintain the same standards, as their better-paid neighbours. Sadly, many of them found themselves pushed off towards the mudflats of society, unable indefinitely to continue to stay afloat. This book is for those people. They were very far from being the cowed, tremulous types one might assume they were. If they chose not to make a fuss, to shut their mouths tightly and just plough on, they usually had their reasons. Reasons born of lifetimes of experience which told them that rocking the boat could only lead to capsize. I was constantly amazed by their determination, their sheer grit, and more than that by their almost unbelievable optimism and *joie de vivre*. This book is a tribute to that extraordinary, captivating, uplifting, sometimes baffling human spirit.

All names and some locations have been changed in order to protect the privacy of the people described. One of my greatest concerns while writing this book was that some of them might recognise themselves in the detail. I only hope that if any of them do, they will accept the description in the spirit in which it is offered – one of heartfelt admiration.

I

KEEPING BODY AND SOUL

I'm sitting in the upstairs room of the job centre at the Oval, and it's crowded. I've come for an interview which is due to start in twenty minutes' time, but I can't imagine what all these other people are doing here. There are about thirty of them, mostly black, various races, crammed on to a few rows of red fake-leather-covered seats. The Brits are identifiable by their slick hairstyles, their streetwise clothes and their broad London twang: 'Orite, Sheila?' 'Yeah, keeps ya off da street, dannit?' There's a big woman of about forty who seems to be South American – she's chatting in Spanish to a younger woman who's probably a student, young with long hair and a trendy rucksack at her feet. The student has a Japanese friend with her, but most of the rest, I'd guess, are African. To my left, an older man talks quietly to a woman sitting beside him, in a language I don't recognise. Everyone seems comfortable, in their milieu, but I'm looking around me, a bit nervous. I'm meant to see someone called Surinder, but I haven't spotted her yet. Suddenly, a scuffle breaks out. The African man to my left is shouting at the South American woman. Dirty looks are being thrown. A door bursts open and a woman appears. Surinder, her name badge announces. 'Boys and Girls!' she shouts, schoolmistressy, calling us to heel. 'Please, form an orderly queue!' She rearranges us with practised speed, pressing me into service as a buffer between the warring parties. Only then does it dawn on me that all these people want to work for Casna Cleaning Services.

Two hours later, I make it into the interview room. By then, the African man next to me has been sent home, told to turn up next week at Hackney job centre with his passport. I don't have my passport either, but Surinder's told me that's OK – I can fax it at the weekend. After all I'm white, is the subtext. The Japanese student has been in and come out minutes later, laughing incredulously. 'Night work!' she says. 'Is night work!' I've spent ages memorising a complicated CV, but I needn't have bothered. The interviewer, whose name is Eileen, barely looks up from her paperwork. Casna needs people who'll stick around, she says. I won't walk out after a couple of days, will I? No, I say. What else does she expect? 'OK, be at the Royal Lancaster Hotel eleven o'clock Monday night, bring your own rubber gloves, wear black tights, black skirt, black shoes, white blouse,' she fires out, reading from the sheet in front of her. I stare at her blankly. 'Does that mean I've got the job?' 'Yes, yes, I'm giving you the job,' she retorts, impatient now. 'Cleaning in four and five star hotels, all outwork, all nights. Four pounds an hour.' 'What's outwork?' I ask. 'Don't ask me,' she says. 'I'm just a freelance. I've only been doing this job a few days.'

I must admit I'm pleased with myself. I've got the first job I applied for, one of about half a dozen at or around the minimum wage advertised today in the job centre. Now I just need to find accommodation. The cards in the shop windows offer shared rooms from about £45 a week, but I'm determined to get a bedsit. Working five nights a week, eleven till seven, I reckon I should take home about £140. I allow myself up to a maximum of £80 for rent. After deducting £9.50 for a bus pass, that will leave £50 a week for food. I buy a copy of *Loot*. There are a few agencies advertising 'Bedsits from £70 a week', but all I get is answering machines. I leave a mobile number, but no one phones back. There are one or two ads for bedsits in my price range, and eventually a woman answers on one of the numbers. The bedsit in Streatham has gone, she says, but her husband has another one not far away. It's £65 a week.

Strathley Road is a semi-gentrified street of bay-fronted terraces. I glimpse Mediterranean colours in living-rooms; people-carriers are parked by the kerb. But number seventy-two has a foul, putrid smell. Two or three flies are suspended above its front door, hovering lazily. I peer into the front window. It's boarded up on the inside. Spiders' webs hang between glass and plywood like shrouds. It's too late to leave, though, because a silver Mercedes is pulling up outside the gate. A small, elderly Asian man emerges, dressed in a greenish tweed suit. There's something quiet, scholarly, about him. He smiles apologetically as he opens the front door and leads the way up a grimy staircase. The 'bedsit' is next to the toilet, about eight foot by eight. There's a sagging single bed, a dilapidated fridge and cooker and a battered 1950s cylindrical water-heater. I take a deep breath. The smell isn't quite so bad up here. 'I'll take it,' I say. We drive to the cashpoint in his car so I can draw out £260 – two weeks' deposit and two weeks' rent, cash not cheque please. The car radio is reporting that Jeffrey Archer has just been convicted of perjury and perverting the course of justice. That's good news, the landlord says. I hand over the cash and he writes a receipt on a pad advertising a drug company. I guess, correctly I find out later, that he's a GP. He doesn't want to give me his name. 'Just ask for "land-lord" if you have to call.' Back inside, my few things un-packed, I survey my surroundings. Even after an afternoon spent brushing and wiping, the overwhelming colour is brown. Brown, dusty industrial carpet. Brown wardrobe, some sort of plywood. Brown curtains. Brown plastic-seated wooden chair. Brown sludge in the bottom of the sink, which refuses to empty. The smell is mustard yellow, though. A hot, liquid yellow which seeps up the stairs and under my door in little, malodorous spurts. I decide to leave the bathroom till later. It's time to prepare for my first night at work.

New girl

After three bus journeys which take a couple of hours, I arrive early at the meeting-point, which is the staff canteen of the Royal Lancaster Hotel in Lancaster Gate. I'm clutching my newly-bought rubber gloves and a piece of paper from Casna which tells me where and when to meet. It's only twenty-past ten, so I sit down to wait. At quarter to eleven, a couple of young girls come in wearing tight white T-shirts, black mini-skirts and white denim jackets. They're carrying rubber gloves and pieces of paper. Then a couple of older women, one by one. Then finally, at quarter to twelve, three managers from Casna. Samuel, who's in his thirties and speaks with an African accent, seems to be in charge. There's also Marge, a Londoner in her fifties with a hacking smoker's cough. She's the only other white person here, apart from me. Samuel sits down and launches into a twenty-minute lecture about reliability. This is obviously a key Casna Thing. More interesting, though, is the brief summary of our pay and conditions. Tonight will be an unpaid training night, though we will be reimbursed if we stay six weeks. There will also be a one-off £10 deduction for setting up a bank transfer facility. No one gets paid unless they have a bank account. If we leave without proper notice – he doesn't say how long this is – our pay will be cut to £3.60 per hour. As he speaks, I can feel my first week's budget crumbling beneath me. Instead of taking home £140, I won't get much more than £100. I'm cheating, of course. I won't actually be paid for four weeks, but I've re-solved to try to live on what I earn each week. That won't be possible now – I'll have to try to repay some next week.

The lecture over, everyone gets a name badge – 'Casna Cleaning Services. Fran' – and a piece of paper with the name of their hotel on. Mine says: 'Your work number is ... 1712. Your hotel is ... SAVOY.' Finally, we all go out into the night and I set off with Marge in her car. But half-way to the Savoy she gets a message on her phone and tells me there's been a change of plan. There's a problem at one of Casna's other hotels, and I'm to help out there tonight. 'One of the women hasn't turned up,' Marge explains with an air of weary disgust. 'You know what she's doing? She's working two jobs at once. She said to me, "Marge, me want three nights." But I told her, she had to work four nights.' She gives me the strong impression that Casna can't be doing with people who have two jobs at once. No matter how low the wages, they're supposed to be enough. Total commitment is required. Marge also warns me of the perils of sleeping on the job, another common problem with Casna's somewhat wobbly workforce. But, she adds, what they don't realise is they're all on camera all the time. Casna always knows.

We arrive at my temporary workplace where I'm handed a burgundy-coloured tabard to put over my white blouse. Then I'm introduced to Esther, a portly, cheerful Ghanaian woman who, Marge tells me with pride, is a real Casna veteran. She's been with the company for nine months, quite an achievement. Marge departs, and Esther takes me down to the staff changing-rooms. Cleaning these two long shed-like basements will be my main job for tonight. The men's are filthy. There are pools of urine all over the floor, dotted with bits of sodden toilet paper. There's obscene graffiti all over the walls of the cubicles, and several of the toilets are blocked. Esther shows me the mops, brushes and bin bags. Then, training over, she leaves me to get on with the job. I must empty the bins, pick up the rubbish from the floor before sweeping and mopping, then clean all the sinks, mirrors and toilets. Then I have to do the same thing all over again in the ladies'. It's indescribably hot down here, but even if it wasn't I'm sure I'd still be sweating copiously. I have to race through the work to finish, as ordered, by break-time at three o'clock. There isn't the faintest hope of catching even a couple of minutes' sleep. Still, I'm rewarded when Esther reappears. 'You're trying,' she says. I glow with pride. She tells me break is forty-five minutes, but Casna deducts an hour's pay for it so we will take an hour. In some hotels they give you food, she says, but not here.

We get a cup of tea and sit down in the canteen, where we're joined by Jean-Pierre, who is introduced by Esther as 'my brother' – a fellow West African. Esther tells me she's been in England nine years, but Jean-Pierre has just been here six months. He's come from France, where he's lived for years, to learn English. He plans to go back there once his studies are complete. He isn't really a cleaner, he explains. In France he's a politician – a socialist councillor. He has grown-up kids and runs a business importing clothing from Thailand to West Africa. That's why he needs to improve his English. I'm sure Jean-Pierre isn't making this up – in the entire time I work for Casna, I never meet anyone who identifies themselves as a cleaner. This isn't just an affectation. Almost everyone is a student of some kind, or is saving money for some planned venture, though quite how anyone can save on these wages I never manage to fathom.

Jean-Pierre tells me his kids were born in France, and he has citizenship there. He can't wait to go back. In France, he says, black and white people live together, but here they live in ghettoes. Here, he can't walk into a pub without feeling everyone's staring at him. He never wears his African clothes outside the house in London. He's horrified, too, by the sight of Muslim women wearing hijab on the streets here. That would never happen in France, he says. Then he makes two V-signs with his fingers and makes a diamond with them around his eyes, to depict a woman with just a slit to see through. Then he laughs uproariously, infectiously. If you choose a new country you must take on its customs, he says, more serious now. Soon we're arguing cheerfully over the extent to which immigrants should have to assimilate, and by the time break is over we're firm friends. I'm sorry I won't be working here full-time, but Esther says if I don't like the Savoy I can come back. After break I have to clean the guests' toilets then the main stairs and reception; dusting, sweeping, mopping, vacuuming. These last few hours drag, though. My back is starting to ache and I'm uncomfortably conscious of my knees. At seven o'clock we change into our street clothes – Jean-Pierre looks for all the world like an advertising executive or PR man in a well-cut wool jacket he certainly didn't buy on his current wages – and we stumble out into the sharp morning air. I'm walking towards the bus stop but sleep is rushing over me in big waves. As soon as I sit down, I'm asleep. Changing buses at the Elephant and Castle, I'm faintly surprised to see that the world is carrying on in its normal, daytime way. The air around me is a whirl of pre-work bustle, everyone freshly shaved and pressed. It's no time since I was part of it, but now I sit separate, waiting unwashed and tired for the bus which will take me in the opposite direction from the incoming commuters. I finally arrive back at the bedsit and fall asleep on my narrow, saggy bed. But the house is awaking now, and the ancient plumbing is whooping and gurgling as the other residents perform their ablutions. By late morning I'm wide awake and feeling as though I've survived some sort of endurance test. I marvel at the stamina of the armies of people who do this night after night, year after year.

Savoy

That night I spend another couple of hours on a series of buses retracing my steps back to the Royal Lancaster. This time the Casna managers arrive soon after eleven, and there are no more hitches. Marge whisks me off to my permanent job at the Savoy, where we arrive, appropriately it seems to me, just as the fingers on the security guard's clock approach midnight. Entering through a dark rabbit-hole in the side of the building, we are plunged without ceremony into a gloomy, subterranean world where cockroaches thrive, drains cough enigmatically and ancient paint peels quietly, endlessly away. Here in the intestines of this huge building, miles of corridors are lined by unimaginable lengths of convoluted piping and sagging wiring, countless kitchens reveal tottering piles of soiled dishes left over from the night's revels and huge bins spill out foothills of dirty linen. So vast is this underbelly that it seems entirely possible one or two of the white dinner-jacketed figures to be seen flitting here and there are not waiters at all, but some remnants of a bygone age, lost and condemned to wander aimlessly from banqueting-room to kitchen, kitchen to ballroom.

Here, by a small, dank hole under a flight of stairs which serves as the cleaners' home base, I'm introduced to my supervisor, Anna, a beautiful, tall woman from Benin with arms so slender and delicate that I fear they could all too easily snap under the strain of a heavy vacuum cleaner or even a too-large yard brush. Here, too, is Sergio, a Venezuelan youth with a huge, warm smile, and Amos, a tall thirty-something from Uganda with a goatee beard, who nods and says, 'Hi.' As we arrange ourselves for our night's work, a cockroach scuttles out from the wall of the cleaning store and Amos lifts his foot to crush it. Then he stops, thinks for a minute and lets it go on its way unharmed. 'Ach, it has its own life to lead,' he says ruminatively.

Armed with the buckets, rags and bottles of all-purpose soap solution which are the stock-in-trade of the Casna cleaner, we head, as one, for a service lift which will take us up into the main hotel. This, it transpires, is one of a series of magical shafts joining the Mr Hyde lurking under the Savoy to the Dr Jekyll above. To emerge through their sliding doors is to burst forth into a fantasia of 1920s opulence so extraordinary that the light seems to hurt your eyes. Here, every art deco cliché is played out in a vast range of custom-designed carpets, in acres of pink marble, in sudden, surprising asides – a walnut-veneered lift or a carefully crafted light fitting. I spend my first night cleaning function rooms, each of which has its own Gilbert and Sullivan-styled name: Pinafore, Mikado, Gondoliers. Pinafore is my favourite, with its warm wood panels swathed in silver studding which swirls and loops around its perimeter. In each room I must first check for rubbish then wipe or dust every surface before hoovering the vast expanse of carpet from end to end. It's not unpleasant work, and there's a constant, faintly romantic strain of evenings recently passed by now-slumbering guests. Clues lie scattered around – a trail of purple feathers, discarded notes for a dull speech about cutlery, a single yellow post-it note with 'Lord MacLaurin' scrawled on it. I almost expect to hear faint echoes of jazz, or maybe a string quartet.

At two in the morning we take a break, queuing in one of the hotel kitchens for chicken nuggets or stew with chips then carrying it through the maze of corridors to the staff canteen. We can heat our food in a microwave when we get there if we want, but no one bothers. This place, which forms the centre of social interaction for the Savoy night cleaners, is ironically named 'The Oasis'. It's a fairly standard canteen with green plastic seats welded to its formica tables so you have to climb into them, and it's currently being decorated so our food is spiced by the overpowering smell of paint. But what makes it so un-oasislike is the mess. We eat every night among the accumulated debris of the long-departed daytime staff, and we have to clear and wipe the tables before we can use them. As we finally tuck into our cold food I notice a mouse ambling casually along the side of the room. I point it out to Sergio and he looks at me with scorn. 'But of course,' he says. 'There are many, many mice here.'

Sergio, who's twenty-one, has been in London just a few months. At home he's a hairdresser and beauty consultant, and at the moment he's taking a full-time English language course. He lives with a community of nuns on the outer reaches of North London, and just has time at the end of his shift for a quick shower before college starts at nine. He's hoping to take a full-time fashion course once his National Insurance number comes through. This sounds like a mere formality, but as the weeks wear on, an increasing part of Sergio's limited leisure time will be expended on this and on his immigration status. His mother is Spanish, he explains, so he should be treated as a European citizen. That means he shouldn't have to pay so much in college fees. He's been told the best way to get his visa sorted out is to sleep outside the office overnight, but of course he can't do that because he works at night. Sometimes he goes off down there at seven, when he finishes work, but there's always a different problem. The queues are too long, it's the wrong day, he's not brought the right paperwork. It never seems to get him down. He just sets a day to try again. And again. It's proving expensive, too. He has to pay a £100 fee, plus lawyer's costs in Spain to sort out the paperwork there. Sergio is particularly keen to get through the bureaucracy, though, because then he says he can apply for a council flat. He's so full of optimism I haven't the heart to tell him how remote are his chances of getting one.

He also mentions another reason why he needs to clear up his immigration status. In term time, foreign students aren't allowed to work more than twenty hours a week. We both agree this is a ludicrous rule. It seems fair enough that people on student visas should have to attend college for a certain number of hours. But if the workforce here is any indication, there must be vast numbers who could never, ever afford to study in the UK without working long hours to support themselves. In all my time with Casna, I never hear a student suggesting he's really in the UK for the money. I never hear one say he'd like to stay on permanently. Far from it, my student colleagues, in the main, are a pretty homesick bunch. What little spare time they have is spent meeting people from 'home', precious pounds are expended on phoning parents or other loved ones. The minute they get their hard-earned certificates they'll be off, hoping for a better life, more respect, in their own countries.

Sergio isn't the only one who puts in a full day at college when he finishes work here. Amos has just finished an engineering degree and he's about to embark on a masters' in particle physics. He lives in Tottenham with his aunt. While he and Sergio travel north each morning, Anna goes east, to Newham. She, too, has just time for a quick wash before dashing out to her college, where she's taking business studies. Anna shares a house with a group of others from Benin, and she's been here nearly a year. Her work number is 810, I've noticed. Mine is 1712. No wonder Casna has to recruit almost daily around the London job centres, I reflect. Tonight, though, no one's complaining, and I'm the only new recruit. The atmosphere in the canteen is jovial, and Amos is teasing Anna gently about her capacity for hard work. 'An-*na*,' he calls her. 'The wonderful, warm and in-de-*fa*-tigable Anna.'

My new companions want to know about me, too.

'Where you from?'

'Manchester.'

'What, Manchester in *England*?' (Later, the Greek security guard will tell me: 'What? You from England? But we *never* have English people working here!')

'So what do you do?'

I'm floored by this question. I say well, I suppose I'm a cleaner.

Wrong answer. Shocked expressions.

'What, you not a student? Fran, you have to study!'

Next question: 'What kind of church do you go to?'

'Er, I don't go to church. I'm not a Christian.'

'What are you, then?'

'I'm not anything.'

More shocked expressions. Later Sara, a quiet, dignified woman from the Congo who doesn't say much, questions me earnestly about why there are so many huge churches in London when no one seems to want to worship in them. When I ask her which church *she* goes to, she tells me she's a Muslim. Anna, for her part, embarks on a mission to bring me to God. 'Fran, you have to talk to Jesus!' she will shout after me down a corridor as a sort of postscript to a list of instructions. 'Clean the fitness centre! Don't forget to mop the floors! Tell God all your troubles and He will make them go away!'

My failure to answer these vital questions correctly, along with the fact that I am the only English cleaner to cross the threshold, to my knowledge, during my month-long sojourn, makes me something of a puzzle. One by one, my colleagues reach their own conclusions as to why I'm here. After a few days I tell Anna in passing that I have a boyfriend who lives in London, and she says, 'Ah, so *that's* why you're here.' She seems happy with that. Amos, for his part, takes to sounding me out on a sometimes bizarre range of topics. At five to seven one morning, as I'm fighting my way through waves of sleep to put my bucket and vacuum cleaner away in the store, he suddenly asks me: 'Fran, do you think Britain should join the Euro?' I answer vaguely that it depends on the economic circumstances but if it's a success I think we'll have to go in eventually. He leans on a brush as he looks at me for a moment, his eyes narrowing slightly. Then he nods, sagely. 'Like all of us,' he says. 'Just keeping body and soul.'

'Keeping body and soul', as Amos so eloquently puts it, is all any of us can expect to do on £4 an hour. Every morning, as we change into our street clothes in the dingy cupboard under the stairs, I'm astonished afresh by the resourcefulness of my colleagues. While I wear only the scruffiest jeans and T-shirts, they all arrive at work and leave again in clothes which are clean, neat and freshly pressed. I wonder constantly at their ability to buy clothes at all, let alone to pay launderette bills or to keep an iron. Such things clearly matter to them. I spend a large portion of my spare time calculating and recalculating my earnings and how much they leave me to spend, and I suspect my colleagues do likewise. I soon learn that even after the first week is past, with its deductions for training and for payroll costs, I won't be taking home as much as I'd expected. For one thing, breaks are unpaid. For another, the hours aren't eleven till seven, as advertised, but twelve till seven. So I only get paid for six hours a night. Thirty hours a week, not forty. About £110, take home. On the plus side, though, I'm putting in lots of overtime. Sometimes I'm asked to come in early to clean offices, sometimes we don't finish our work till eight or even later. Also, I've discovered I'm entitled to some Housing Benefit and I factor that into my budget, though none of my colleagues can do so, of course.

Lily

Life at Strathley Road begins to form a pattern. Home from work for a few hours' sleep, then awake before lunchtime. I have to hope someone has left some hot water, as the bathroom meter only takes old 50p pieces and I don't have any. If they haven't, I have to run back and forth between bedsit and bathroom, filling the bath from kettles and bowls. This has to be done swiftly, as the bath plug has a hole in it. The whole exercise takes on a rather comic, *It's a Knock-Out* sort of air, marred only by the distinctly un-comic task of removing my house-mates' blobs of shaving foam and bits of soggy tissue from the sink each day. Once dressed, I have a bowl of economy cereal before heading out to do the day's shopping. This has to be done daily, as the fridge is barely working and the August weather is hotting up. I soon discover that budget shopping is much easier for a large family or group than it is for one   the only way to get cheap food is to buy in bulk, which is clearly not an option for me. I find myself dragging up and down the high street, trying to get the best price on a single pepper or a couple of bananas. So my choice is severely restricted. For one whole week I eat suppers of nothing but pasta with pesto, and for another, baked potatoes with cheese or tuna. I don't go hungry, though. I find I can get eight chocolate bars for eighty pence, and anyway there's always my night-time meal. The hot weather does nothing to improve the smell, which I fear may be coming from the drains. The sink in my room remains resolutely blocked, despite a major outlay of £3.50 on something called 'Drainbuster'. I mention it to the landlord, and he suggests I lean out of my first-floor window to dismantle the drainpipe. I'm not tempted.

I don't see a lot of my house mates at first, though I hear them clumping up and down the stairs on their way to or from work. Gradually, though, I get on to nodding terms with them. There's a Brazilian couple who seem to run some sort of barbecueing business, and who constantly cart equipment in and out of the house. There's a cheerful English man with a pit-bull terrier, a quiet Asian couple and a French student who knocks on my door one evening, in a quandary about how he is supposed to get hot water for a bath. I continue to wonder, though, about the downstairs front room. As the smell is at its worst just outside there, I suspect it has fallen prey to the disastrous drainage situation. Quite suddenly one afternoon, the mystery resolves itself. There's a knock on my door and when I open it, there is the smell. To be more precise, there is a rather pale, frail old woman, from whom the smell is emanating. She's holding out a brightly painted porcelain statuette, which seems to depict some sort of rabbit.

'Would you like to have this?' she asks. 'Only I'm being evicted and I'm frightened it will get broken in the move. It's quite valuable, you know.'

There is really no delicate way to describe Lily. She's wearing what was probably once a white sweatshirt, but which is now grey and liberally smeared with what turns out to be cat-shit, as if she's been wiping dirty hands across her chest. Some brown liquid has seeped upwards from the hem and has soaked the bottom eight or nine inches of the material. Her crimplene trousers, which hang low over her hips and buttocks, are probably no cleaner but being brown (I think) are a little easier to deal with. The ensemble is topped by a headscarf, from under which wisps of dirty grey hair are escaping. I decline her offer politely, explaining that I have to move soon myself, and that I'd be afraid of breaking her treasured ornament. She's out of breath from climbing the stairs, and she accepts my offer of a seat. She doesn't want a cup of tea, though, which is fortunate as my only spare mug has been pressed into service to bail the sludge out of the bottom of my sink. 'The landlord wants me out,' she says. 'He says all the other residents are complaining about the smell. But it was my poor kitty that caused it, and I had to have her put down last week.' Gradually, the truth begins to dawn on me. 'You mean you live downstairs?' I ask, incredulous. 'In the boarded-up room?'

'It's not boarded up!' she exclaims, indignant now. 'Those are shutters. I had them put up after I was attacked in the street, because it made me so nervous.' It turns out she's been here for years. For a long time she had no electricity, and she still has no running water. I don't even want to think what she does for a bathroom – that's on the first floor and the stairs are obviously too much of a trial for her to attempt them regularly.

I take to Lily instantly, despite the smell. I feel guilty for getting so cross about it, and relieved that I haven't got round to mentioning it to the landlord. She says she comes from York, and I tell her I had a lovely time when I lived there. She smiles and says, 'I'm so glad,' as if she means it. The landlord is a terrible man, she says. He comes round and shouts at her, and once when the council overpaid her housing benefit he kept the money then blamed her when they asked for it back. Now she can't claim the benefit any more because the council is adamant she owes it money. And the landlord doesn't look after the place, though it's better now than it was when squatters took over the upstairs. Then there was nothing but noise and drinking, she says. I say it sounds like a good thing she's being evicted because now the council will have to rehouse her, but she's not convinced. For one thing, she says, she's had trouble with the council and she's nervous of having to deal with them. For another, she only pays £40 a week here and she might have to pay more somewhere else. Also, she's been here a long time and she really doesn't want to move. She thinks if she can just tidy up enough the landlord will let her stay. That's why she's been throwing out so much junk. She says her friend is going to help her deal with the landlord. I say if that doesn't work out, I'll see if I can do anything.

A few days later I pay Lily a call to see how things are. I knock, and then wait for several minutes while she hauls herself to her feet and navigates her way over to the door. I can hear her panting, knocking into things and muttering 'Damn, damn,' under her breath. When she finally does open up, I can see immediately why it's taken so long. Her room is only about twelve feet square, and every single surface is covered with debris and litter. The walls are lined from floor to ceiling with books. There are books and magazines all over the floor, in heaps and piles. Mingling with them is an assortment of other junk – old food cartons, clothes, waste paper. There isn't a right-angle visible anywhere. I literally can't see the floor at all. The smell is fierce – and it must be better now than it was, for since the cat died it's receded down the stairs. Now it just hovers malignantly in the hallway. She doesn't ask me in, to my relief, but peering round the door I realise there's no bed, just a lumpy old chaise-longue which is barely visible, like everything else in the room. She explains that she's been tidying up in the hope that the landlord will see her efforts and relent. She's managed to give the rabbit to the man with the dog, but now she's worrying about a two-foot high porcelain penguin which she's placed hopefully in the front hall. Lily tells me she paid £27 for it at a charity sale, and asks if I'd like to have it. Actually it's quite a novelty, but I don't feel I can take it and on my budget I can hardly offer to pay her.

I ask whether her friend has been able to help at all and it seems she hasn't, so I offer to give Age Concern a ring. She agrees, but doesn't seem much cheered. 'I'm just hoping I'll go to sleep one night and not wake up,' she says. I say surely there must be something to live for and she says no, not since the cat was put down. I'm silenced. I can't think of anything cheering to say.

I phone Age Concern, though, and have a long chat with a very nice man who makes a lot of helpful suggestions about benefits to which Lily might be entitled. He concludes by saying that if she doesn't want to move, no one should try to make her. That includes the landlord, and it's possible action could be taken to get him to provide her with some proper facilities. We agree that I should get Lily to call and make an appointment to see someone – which, to my surprise, she does without hesitation. She comes back from her meeting full of enthusiasm. She's spent six hours with a counsellor, who's going to talk to the local authority about her benefits and also fix her up with a taxi service to go to and from the shops. They'll also help her to deal with the landlord, if he takes his eviction threat forward.

By now, Lily and I are the best of friends. Unknowingly she's helped me a lot. I can't say living in an eight-foot-square room with a blocked sink becomes a pleasure but it becomes much more bearable, knowing she's there. Now I feel more grounded. Imperceptibly, the place is beginning to feel like a home, now I have a neighbour I can talk to. Even the bugs in my room seem more friendly than threatening, somehow. They're not biting bugs, just little brown beetles shaped like tiny cockroaches. I'm re-reading *Down and Out in Paris and London*, and I'm mildly shocked when I get to the bit where Orwell writes about having to throw away a whole pan of milk because a bug falls in it. I'm certainly not so fastidious, and I'm becoming less so by the day. If I find mould on top of my tomato sauce or my bread rolls, I just pick it off and carry on regardless. Nor do I suffer any ill-effects from this.

'Foreign shit'

At work, too, I'm beginning to feel I know where I belong. And surprisingly, I've discovered the Casna cleaners are not the lowest creatures in the carefully calibrated hierarchy which exists in the bowels of the Savoy. That distinction must be reserved for the men with overalls and wellingtons who hose out the kitchens after the evening service ends. We find them there each night as we queue for our chips and stew, often splashing through pools of the thick grey water they're slooshing into the drains. They have to scrape away the accretions of grease and slime left on the cookers by countless top-class dinners, and – worst of all – they have to empty the waste disposal unit. This involves filling a small, wheeled skip with indescribable brown sludge, sometimes garnished charmingly by a lobster claw which pokes through the surface, or a few salad leaves, scraped belatedly from a left-behind plate after the unit's been cleaned. The person who does this job then has to wheel this bubbling morass through a maze of sweltering, stinking corridors and negotiate at least two service lifts on his way to the rubbish room, which is about the only place in the hotel smellier than the skip's festering contents. This is one of the hardest places to find, tucked away in a far corner of the basement, and I regularly get lost looking for it. Some nights, though, I find I can literally follow my nose – the mixed aroma of rotting vegetables and drains is quite unmistakable.

We see the welly men, too, in the canteen as we eat our dinner. They follow us up there, carrying plates of whatever we've left behind, but only Sara sits with them. Anna says they're Nigerians. Funny people, Nigerians, she says, wrinkling her nose. Sally, a Zimbabwean and one of the many new recruits who comes and goes again within days, agrees with her. Most of these men are quiet, absorbed in their food, but one is a garrulous man of about thirty who turns out to be not from Nigeria but from Abidjan, in Côte d'Ivoire. He doesn't eat but he chain-smokes – cigarettes sustain him better than food, he says with a serious face. He rolls his own, five or six during his hour's break. Anna makes a point of sitting on the other side of the canteen but he just raises his voice and carries on, addressing the world at large.

We should all count ourselves lucky, the man from Abidjan says. This night cleaning lark is child's play. Some of his friends work right round the clock to try to save some money in London. One of them goes to work all night then travels round and round on the Circle Line for two hours, catching a nap before he goes to his day job. Sometimes he's so tired he even sleeps on the streets. 'You know how the white people sometimes lie on the pavements? He does that,' he says, putting up his two hands, palms forward, and throwing back his head in imitation of a man lying on his back.

Above us, there's a complex social structure. Next up from us in the hierarchy is the night porter, an ageing Scot called Bill. He often wanders over for a chat while I'm cleaning the reception. Bill's been here for donkey's years – so long that he even talks with a cockney accent. He's kept a mental list of all the celebrities whose bags he's had the honour to carry over the years. He usually has a bit of gossip about each of them.

'Go on,' he says. 'Name your favourite singer. I bet they've been here.'

I say Aretha Franklin, and he looks flummoxed. 'Well we had that Shirley Bassey here once,' he says. 'And that Rolf Harris was in last night. But I'm not so sure about him. Australian. They don't tip.'

Although he comes across as quite an austere character, Bill has a surprisingly dry sense of humour. One night I meet him stretching his back after cleaning dozens of pairs of guests' shoes. 'Some of them get a single room then put five pairs out for polishing,' he grumbles. 'Where the 'eck do they think this is? The bleedin' Savoy?'

Bill is rarely ruffled. One morning at about four o'clock, a casually dressed man wanders past the reception desk. Bill runs after him: 'Can I help you, sir?' It quickly becomes obvious that the man is one of the dozens who sleep in the doorways along the Strand. He's of Middle Eastern appearance. 'Where's the toilet?' he asks, but before waiting for the answer he's decided Bill isn't going to be helpful. 'You're shit!' he shouts. 'I'm foreign shit! Just foreign shit! Tell me where is the toilet!' Bill is a little oasis of calm. He stands, motionless and expressionless, for several minutes as the man's stream of invective rises to a crescendo then finally peters out. Then Bill says, quite quietly, 'I'm going to have to ask you to leave now, sir.' And amazingly, he does, throwing back little bursts of abuse back over his shoulder as he goes. The receptionist jokes that he was probably a guest, checking in early. I must say I'd wondered myself at Bill's ability to tell the difference. Although the hotel affects to cater for the English upper classes, most of the guests are foreign and some of them are every bit as scruffy as our night visitor, if not more so.

Somewhere above Bill in the night-time pecking order are the waiters, who drift in and out in white dinner-jackets bringing drinks orders or late-night snacks for guests. Then there are the reception staff, who wear black suits. Only the really senior staff, such as the night manager, get to wear their own clothes. When he comes in, everyone puts their heads down and looks busy. We, of course, wear our own black skirts, white blouses and black shoes – but that's down to economy rather than status. Our true position is marked out by the burgundy-coloured cleaner's tabards we wear over our blouses. Male cleaners, though, are provided with burgundy T-shirts and trousers.

Anna

There's a separate hierarchy, of course, among the Casna staff. At its tip there's the owner, Nick, a pleasant, laid-back chap whose appearance in the cleaning store at around midnight one night causes waves of panic. Why was he here? Did he say anything? Has someone complained? We never find out, and apart from this one apparition we never have anything to do with him. Queries or complaints are dealt with through phone calls to the company's head office in central London, or via the area managers, Marge and Samuel. We underlings don't see much of either of them, as we're usually hard at work when they pay their nightly visits. Most of our contacts with Casna are filtered through Anna.

In recognition of her higher status, Anna is allowed to wear her black skirt and white blouse without a tabard over the top, and she gets a higher hourly rate than the rest of us. But she still has to do her share of the cleaning. To the rest of the world, Anna is just the most senior of the Casna cleaners, one step up from the men in wellingtons. To us, she's the boss. This betwixt-and-between position leaves her unsure whether she's one of us or one of them. Sometimes she's voluble and cheerful, sometimes so astonishingly uncommunicative that it makes the rest of us stretch our eyes in disbelief. In one of these moods, she will take me into a suite of offices, wave an arm airily and disappear without a single word. I'll set to work only to be told later that she's already done half the cleaning in that particular room. Then she'll get angry. Why have I taken so long? Why have I wiped the desks when she's already done them? This apparent disability isn't caused by language difficulties, for she speaks perfect English. Nor is it always the result of tiredness, ill-health or depression. One night, after we line up for our chips and stew, she beckons us all with a twinkle in her eye and leads us out of the kitchen in the direction of the Savoy's riverside function rooms. Once there, still without speaking a word, she indicates we should sit at one of the linen-clad tables to eat. We all look at one another, panic-stricken amid the chandeliers and the ornate plasterwork. Surely we'll all be sacked if we're caught in here? Still, we do as we're told and sit, our hunger frozen by discomfort. And a moment later, our worst fears are realised: the night manager walks in. He smiles cheerfully and asks if we're enjoying our new canteen. It turns out the decorators have closed the 'Oasis' for a day or two. Sergio gives me a significant look. 'It's culture,' he whispers. I really don't have a clue whether this covers it.

When I first arrived, I was struck by Anna's slender beauty and her graceful deportment. I took the gentle ribbing the male staff gave her as a sign of pure affection, even adoration, and failed to detect a slight undercurrent of irony. Sometimes the signs of insubordination are unmistakable, though. In Iqbal, a young Bangladeshi guy, for instance. Iqbal is a little bloke, about twenty but seems younger. I'm surprised to learn he's married with a couple of kids. He and his family live in an overcrowded house in Tower Hamlets with his parents. Iqbal resents having to do as he's told by Anna. One night, he spends most of his break trying to push a piece of paper under her nose. It seems to be some kind of visitor's pass from a security firm. 'You will see, Anna. You will see,' he keeps repeating. Anna takes no notice. Iqbal continues with his ineffectual needling till five minutes before break is due to end, when Anna gets up, shouts: 'OK! Lessgo!' and heads for the door of the canteen. The next night Iqbal is gone, to a new job as a watchman. None of us take his departure too seriously, though. The

Africans all regard Iqbal as something of a joke – he's been in this country nine years, gone to school here, yet his English is still far less fluent, less grammatically perfect than theirs. He has no qualifications at all. What a fool, to have passed up so many opportunities! After he's gone, Amos takes to mimicking his outburst: 'Just because you a prince today, it don' mean you a prince tomorrow. Y'unnerstan my Eenglish?' he will cry, to shrieks of laughter.

There isn't much joy in Anna's life. She lives miles out on the fringes of East London – a bus journey which takes about an hour and a half. After she finishes college in the afternoons she shops, cleans and tries to sleep, but often she comes to work without having been to bed at all. At break, she picks at her food listlessly then pushes her plate aside before putting her head down on her arms and falling asleep. She worries about her family back home, and the only social life she seems to have consists of visits to her house from other West Africans who live in London or who are passing through. She's often ill, sometimes with a cold, sometimes a headache, once a raging toothache which she refuses to have treated – possibly, I guess, because she fears the dentist's bills. But she never misses work. To miss work would mean losing a night's pay. Every morning when she finishes her shift, Anna uses her mobile phone to call her boyfriend back home and make sure he's out of bed so he won't be late for work. Later in the day, he phones her to chat, and if there's worrying news from home she'll borrow the day-old *Daily Telegraph* I purloin from reception each night to see if there's anything on the foreign pages. She's hopes her boyfriend will join her soon – she hasn't been able to afford a visit home – and she scornfully rebuffs any approaches she receives from other men. Poor Amos, who lights upon almost every new female staff member as a potential girlfriend, seems to have had short shrift. 'He asked me out once but I told him, "What are you doing? Why would I go out with you when you are working as a cleaner?"' My feelings about Anna graduate from warm admiration to simmering resentment, and finally to pity. I come to realise that the main emotion which both motivates and paralyses her is fear. Fear of the Casna managers, who come to her with their complaints if everything isn't right. Fear of the housekeeper, who is never seen but who remains a shadowy and threatening figure in all our lives: 'If the housekeeper finds a single speck on this carpet we will have to do it all again,' Anna will threaten, indicating some vast acreage of Wilton. And, saddest of all, fear of us. For Anna, though elevated above her colleagues, hasn't the weight or authority to counter their frequent outbreaks of rebelliousness. She's outnumbered, and she knows it. This, I think, is at the root of her mood swings. She's torn between a need to be feared, and a desperate desire to be liked.

One night, Anna gives me a companion to work with – a big, languid woman from Zambia who laughs at my frantic efforts to clean everything to Anna's satisfaction. Julia lies back on a bench in the Fitness Centre and tells me to take it 'slooow'. 'Don't rush-rush-rush like that! This I learned from my supervisor when I worked at the Café Royal,' she instructs. Over supper, she tells me how she's left her kids, aged sixteen and seventeen, in Sweden with their dad. Sweden is cool, she says, but she doesn't want to bring them to Britain because it's so violent and crime-ridden. Now she lives in Clapton with her boyfriend, who has a good job as a meter reader. She's not at all sure she wants to work for Casna. How many hours a night do we get paid for, she asks? When I tell her it's only six because she won't be paid for breaks she gets up and leaves, saying she doesn't need £24 this badly. As dawn breaks, Anna joins me in the American Bar where I'm polishing tables. 'She your friend now, that woman?' she asks. I confide that as she's just walked out, I don't think I'll be seeing her again. 'She was a lazy woman,' Anna says angrily. 'I think she makes money by bitching.' She pauses for a moment, reflecting. 'In Africa,' she goes on, 'they tell us in England we can make so much money we can buy a house in two weeks. But there's no way to do that. You have to work.' Then she straightens up with a shake of her bony shoulders, brightening. 'But if you really try,' she adds finally, 'You know you can get a rise to four pounds fifty an hour.'

Amos

While Anna clearly struggles to maintain her equanimity in the face of the trials she faces, Amos is altogether more pragmatic more optimistic. He keeps constantly in mind the fact that he has an engineering degree and that this grim existence is only temporary – 'keeping body and soul', as he says.

Amos works six nights a week. He plans to keep this up even when his masters' course starts in a few weeks' time. His aunt, with whom he lives, has other plans. Noting that his degree hasn't done him any good financially so far, she regards his latest plans for self-betterment as nothing but a means of throwing good money after bad. She's presented him with an application form for nursing training. He's wondering half-heartedly whether to fill it in or not. After all, he tells me, the money would be good. I wonder whether to tell him that most people in the UK think nurses are paid an absolute pittance, but I don't.

When Anna has a night off, Amos stands in as supervisor. In this role, too, he takes a far more laid-back attitude. He's conscientious when there's time to do the job thoroughly, but when we're short-staffed – which we often are – he'll tell us to do just what Samuel describes as 'the necessary' – a quick lick and a polish in the places the housekeeper is most likely to look. He views my efforts to prove my cleaning abilities with surprise, even a little admiration. 'I didn't think you could cope but you're really trying. I like that,' he says.

Amos has clearly given some thought to the issue of finding a wife, and has decided that in the circumstances the Savoy is as good a place to start as any. After all, if he spent his one free night a week in the West End surveying the talent, he could wake up the next morning to find his entire week's wages gone. And there's a steady flow of female recruits, most of whom leave after a night or two, wracked by backache and exhaustion or consumed with fury after a run-in with Anna. Each new woman who appears is given the once-over by Amos. He doesn't waste time on those who fail to meet his two main criteria: First, they have to be single. Second, they have to be white, or thereabouts. Amos tells me he's decided he wants to 'marry white'. Anna gives me a knowing look and a poke in the ribs when he says this but I'm unmoved. I dropped out in round one after mentioning casually that my boyfriend lives not far from his aunt's house.

The first likely target who comes on the scene during my time at the Savoy is Wai Li, a diminutive Malaysian student with enormous platform-soled trainers and a very cool mobile phone. Wai Li shares a two-bedroom flat in New Cross with half a dozen other Malaysians, and she's taking a basic English course before going on to study tourism. She's just returned from a month's summer holiday at home and is a Casna veteran, having spent some time working at the hotel I went to on my first night. She remembers Esther and Jean-Pierre with affection – she called Jean-Pierre 'Papa', she says. But she's not destined to form any such warm relationships here, despite Amos's efforts. When he suggests he could take her out on his night off, she doesn't take him remotely seriously. She just giggles briefly, for all the world as if she were convinced he were joking. Amos is floored. With the rest of us there, he isn't in a position to labour the point. Anna laughs and says, 'She won't go out with you. You'd have to go to a dog restaurant. They eat dog in Malaysia.' Wai Li giggles again, neither confirming nor denying the allegation.

Perhaps fortunately for Amos, she's gone within the week. One night I come across her and Anna in some far-flung corridor. There are little angry pink spots high on Wai Li's cheek bones. As soon as she spies me, Anna launches into a sort of third-person, remote-controlled harangue, addressing her remarks to me but clearly hoping I'll back her up in some dispute with Wai Li: 'Ask her! Does she want to clean the toilets? Does she want to clean the fitness centre?' The implication, of course, is that these options would be far worse than whatever it is that Anna wants Wai Li to do – whatever it is she's resisting. 'I am going to call the manager! I am going to call the manager because she is angry!' Anna cries after my retreating back as I make off, uncertain how I'm supposed to respond. When I return to the cleaning store at the end of the shift there's a note to Casna on top of the supervisor's notebook. 'I want to resign from cleaning job! Please send all my money straight away!' And that's the last we hear of Wai Li.

Amos has only slightly more luck with a Czech psychology student called Olga who's come to the UK to learn English during her university holidays. Olga is plump and pretty in a homely way, and by the end of her first night things are starting to look quite positive. It's a quiet shift and we're fully staffed for a change, so by half past six the three of us – me, Amos and Olga, who's been put to work alongside me so I can show her the ropes – are doing some desultory wiping together in the American bar. Amos wants to know all about Prague. 'I could come there to visit you,' he ventures. Then, as if he hadn't already been bold enough, 'Who knows? I might fall in love with you.' There's nothing like the direct approach. Olga smiles warmly, and lets Amos walk her to the tube and show her on to her train before setting off back to catch his own bus home. But these moments of hope are soon revealed to be the fragile bubbles they really are. How could Amos even have dreamed of visiting Olga in Prague? The following night, she reveals he's asked her to go out with him to Leicester Square before work. 'What,' I ask, surprised at his financial audacity, 'in a club?' 'No,' she replies. 'Just to walk around and look.'

Hunger

The offer obviously hasn't been tempting enough, for Olga has turned it down. Perhaps if Amos had been able to suggest a meal he would have been more likely to succeed, for Sergio tells me he's spotted her pinching the greasy, tasteless cheese sandwiches left in the canteen each night in the vain hope that someone will be desperate enough to eat them. She's been slipping them into her bag to eat during the day. Presumably, she's surviving mainly on two o'clock chips and stew. Sergio's revelation doesn't surprise me, for Olga certainly isn't the first. I've been reading through the supervisor's notebook in the few idle moments I can catch alone in the cleaning store. This records any incident during the night, so the Casna managers can catch up on what's been going on. One entry from last year reads: 'Ibrahim had his bag searched by security and they found a banana and some uncooked fish. He was told not to come back here again.'

One of the problems for Casna employees is the long wait for their first pay day. New arrivals from poorer countries, even if they've saved up what may seem like a large sum in their own currency, see their nest-egg disappear virtually overnight when they arrive in London. If they're not lucky enough to have relatives to stay with, they'll probably have to find a room in a shared house, and they'll almost certainly have to pay a couple of months' rent up front. That will come to a minimum of £500. Then, if they want to work, they must pay the £9.50 for a bus pass that will allow them to make a slow journey from their outer-London home to their inner-London job. Small wonder, then, that some of them don't have enough to eat.

I'm pretty sure none of my close colleagues would think of stealing anything more valuable than the odd sandwich, but this doesn't stop them from coming under suspicion. One night at about a quarter to three, just as our break-time is drawing to a close, Marge arrives in the canteen. She sits down with Anna, who's in one of her uncommunicative moods and is sleeping a few tables away from the rest of us. Marge looks grim, and I begin to wonder whether I'm about to be sacked – I shouted at Anna last night for following me around re-wiping the tables in the American Bar after I'd polished them twice already. It's worse than that. After a few minutes, the two of them come over. 'We've got a problem,' Marge says. Apparently, the piano player in the American Bar has been in the habit of leaving his personal CD player behind a curtain near where he sits. Last Friday he forgot to pick it up when he went home, and by Monday evening when he was back on duty it had gone. He doesn't want to make a fuss, and so all the staff in the hotel are being told if it's returned, no more will be said about it. The hotel security already know who took the CD player, Marge says, because it was all captured on camera. I don't feel comforted by this piece of nonsense, and neither does anyone else. After all, if they knew who committed the theft, shouldn't they have sacked them before they nicked something really valuable? We all feel we've been accused of something, and we haven't any proof we didn't do it. After Marge has gone, I remember I dusted that grand piano on Friday night. I even asked Amos for a fresh cloth because mine was making smeary marks on its highly-polished surface. I feel inexplicably guilty. And if I feel like that, I'm sure my colleagues must feel even more so – they know they're in a strange country where people distrust them even before anything happens. For several days, we're left in limbo. As promised, no one says any more about it. Not even whether the CD player was returned or not, or whether the culprit was apprehended. I'm sure Marge, once she's done her bit by passing on the message, doesn't regard it as her job to keep us informed. And there's no one else who really communicates with us at all, so we're left wondering, feeling everyone must be pointing the finger.

Harmonies

Little by little everything gets back to normal, of course, and we relax back into our roles. Now there's a settled nucleus to the team, Anna, Amos, Sergio, Sara and me, and we each have our allotted roles. Each night forms a sort of symphony. At midnight, or just before, we perform our overture in and around the cleaning store. Here we congregate, fix our name badges on to our tabards and sally forth, balancing vacuum cleaners in one hand, buckets in the other. We ascend together in the service lift and burst forth into the American Bar just as the last customers are finishing their drinks, just as the barmen are clearing away their little bowls of nuts and olives and pulling down the shutters on the bar. For the next few hours there's a steady, repeated theme as we warm to our tasks – Sergio in the toilets, me in the reception, Amos polishing floors, the latest arrival cleaning the Fitness Centre.

Sometimes Anna asks us to swap around, but Sara only ever does one task. She cleans an area of the hotel which is formally known as the Thames Foyer, but which is referred to by Casna people simply as 'Sara's Place'. It's regarded by the rest of us with awe, for it involves gargantuan feats of polishing and cushion-plumping. Sara herself remains something of an enigma. Where Anna is tall and slender, she's smaller and her figure is rounded without being plump. Anna straightens her hair, but Sara just keeps hers cropped short. She lives with her sister's family, but worries about the time when she may have to move out and pay a market rent. I never find out where she goes in the daytime, though I'm fairly sure she has things to do because while the rest of us stretch and stumble as the seven o'clock air hits our faces, she's already half way to the bus stop. Sara walks as if she were holding something precious inside her – carefully poised, dainty. Her English is BBC-perfect, spoken with a deep, rich accent. She speaks so rarely that it's always a surprise to hear her voice at all. What she does say is often surprising. One morning as we're changing under the stairs, Sara looks at Anna as if seeing her for the first time: 'Gosh, Anna, your breasts are very small!' Anna takes no offence, but she admits she's lost weight. Sara is right. Even since I arrived, Anna's got thinner.

Visitors, welcome and unwelcome

I'm happy that Anna now trusts me enough to give me my own area to clean. I like the reception because things happen there. Guests drift in and out, men arrive with piles of newspapers in vans, couriers bring in parcels and post. One night U2 arrive after a concert with an entourage of dozens of people in tow. I'm ordered to hide, of course, but still it adds a frisson to the night's work. As I clean the offices behind the reception desk, I can scan the VIP list and gauge each entry by the comment written next to the name: 'Adam Rickitt. Singer. Used to be in *Coronation Street*,' reads one rather icy note. Others qualify not through celebrity but through wealth or through staying power – the chief executive of a sludge-pump company who always uses the Savoy when he's in London, for example. The ones who need no introduction, ones like U2, are the most important, of course. There are extra staff on duty for their arrival.

Most of the guests are American tourists, though. And to the majority of them, the cleaning staff are invisible. There are some who notice our presence as if through a haze, nodding or grunting vaguely as they step around our hoovers or over our legs as we kneel to wipe a skirting board. There are a few who see us more clearly, who even smile and say 'Hello.' To be honest, this makes me jump. I've come to expect people not to really focus on me, and I wonder if these guests are the same with my black colleagues. We hardly have any black guests, of course. Just occasionally, someone will approach me as I dust the reception desk– where can they get a drink at this time of night, can someone bring their bags down from their room as they're expecting a taxi to take them to the airport? I'm very unnerved when this happens. To be honest, I have the feeling I'm not supposed to have anything to do with the guests, though no one has actually said so. They wouldn't need to – in most cases, the chances of one of the cleaners approaching a guest would be extremely slim. Most of my colleagues wouldn't make eye contact, but I sometimes forget myself and look up as they approach. I don't want to take responsibility for their needs, though, and I make haste to find Bill or the receptionist to deal with them. It's partly a matter of uniform, I think. Replace my tabard with a smart black jacket and I'd be ready to face the world. But this scrap of cloth marks me out as a non-speaking person.

The guests aren't the only fellow inhabitants with whom we have an uneasy relationship. The cockroaches become bolder as the night wears on, graduating from short, sharp dashes into the light and back into their crevices to slow, confident ambles down basement corridors before dawn breaks. The mice are happier still after the calm falls, sniffing the carpet of the American Bar for scraps, trotting curiously under the tables in Sara's Place, mooching around the walls of the staff canteen. Sometimes their presence is underlined by entries in the incident log, which is kept in the offices behind reception. One night, after they've been spotted in the River Restaurant and the Lincoln Room, the night receptionist suggests 'a blitz' while the hotel is quiet. Later the same evening, he adds that he's seen a mouse running under the door of one of the bedrooms. He fears they're invading the hotel floors now, he says, and he suggests that if the situation is to continue perhaps the doors should be altered so the creatures can't get underneath them.

A bad job

In the reception, untoward things rarely happen. The air of calm radiated by Bill and the other staff there stills my constant anxiety about whether I've got the carpets really clean, whether I've left an ashtray unemptied. And at around six o'clock I can go outside into the cool morning and polish the brass on the front of the hotel. After vacuuming and wiping frantically all night, it feels like taking a break. Even sweeping the pavement in the little street that leads up to the hotel from the Strand is a pleasure. As I gather up my little piles of cigarette ends and gumwrappers, the taxi-drivers who congregate on the corner will crack jokes for me: 'Ow much will it cost me to get yer rahnd my ahse to do that?' 'Oh, about thruppence. It'd be more than I get here.'

So I'm resentful when I'm asked occasionally to do another area. The toilets, for example. It's not that I object in principle to cleaning toilets, or even that most of the work is particularly unpleasant. Downstairs in the basement where the ballrooms are, I don't really have to do anything I don't do at home. Perhaps the incidence of dried-up vomit is a little higher, but even scraping up this mess isn't so terrible. What I really object to, though, is the gents' next to Sara's Place. Aesthetically, it's stunning – all pink marble, gleaming chrome, black tiles and bevelled glass – brand new but in perfect harmony with the hotel's art deco theme. But the man who designed the urinals – and I'm sorry, but it had to be a man – has put a frosted-glass panel into the front of each stall, presumably to catch splashes. Not only do these panels, of which there are about thirty, signally fail to do their job – I have to kneel on a urine-damp floor in front of each one as I clean it – but they also require hand cleaning, first with a green scourer, then with a cloth, then with a duster. Each time I do this job, dizzy from the ammonia fumes, I fantasise about bringing the designer down here and pushing *his* head into the bottom of twenty urinals, one by one. Sergio regularly incurs Anna's wrath by using his mop to do this job at arm's length, but I'm not so brave.

The worst job of all is the American Bar. I hate that bar with a vengeance. It's a kind of tacky 1980s pastiche of what passed for art deco at the time. Its dark blue carpet has one of those patterns involving beige semi-circles intersected with straight lines. Ghastly, badly-drawn pictures of Audrey Hepburn and of Liza Minelli in *Cabaret* are framed by mirror-tiled panels which are always smeared because we have to clean them with damp rags – presumably Casna regards Windolene as an unnecessary expense. They charge £10 for a cocktail in here and to compensate they put out little bowls of crisps, nuts and olives. It is staggering what the clientele can do with a single crisp. A few crumbs between the sofa cushions (this is on housekeeper's 'top ten hits' list – woe betide the cleaner who doesn't get underneath here for a look), a few placed strategically on the clumpy wooden tripod which holds the cheap black vinyl table's one wooden leg steady, after a fashion. The rest can be liberally stamped into the carpet. I swear I scrub that carpet with the brush attachment of the vacuum cleaner till there isn't a single speck on it. But half an hour later the little buggers have crept out from between the fibres and are all standing to attention for the supervisor's visit. Even Amos makes me clean this carpet over and over again. No one ever seems to bother about the huge white stain in the middle of it, which looks as if it's been witness to a flour-and-water attack. Or, for that matter, the ink blots on the cushions, or the smears on the mirror-tiles. We aren't paid to worry about those.

The point about cleaning, you see, is that you must cover your back. In this job, no one will ever thank you for taking a pride in your work, for an absence of dirt is never noticed. No, the smart cleaner has quite a different strategy. Anna tells me one night, laughing, how one cleaner here worked out that the housekeeper only checked the dusting of high-level objects such as pictures, so he did those carefully then slept for two hours each night. I have to admit I'm not a clever cleaner, though my tendency to clean things because they're dirty does lessen as the weeks pass. After a while, I figure out that if something's really grimy that's because it *never* gets cleaned. And the only plausible explanation for that is that the housekeeper doesn't care. I'm surprised at myself now when I remember how I climbed on a chair to dust the glass shelves and the ornaments at the end of one of the ballrooms on my first night – no one had touched them for weeks, I could see. At that early stage in my cleaning career, I half believed someone would notice the special effort I'd made and would give me credit for it. But that was nonsense, of course. No, the things you have to look out for are the things that are clean even though you haven't been cleaning them. That means the last cleaner who passed through here took care to do them, and there's usually a reason for that. In the reception, for example, the little pieces of wood between each small glass window are always clean. In the Fitness Centre, they're left dirty, presumably because the housekeeper checks the reception more carefully than the Fitness Centre. There are an infinite number of things that can be cleaned in any building, of course, so the cleaners' world is rich with opportunities for tyranny. I don't know who calls the housekeeper to account if the place isn't clean. I only know she kicks Anna, and Anna kicks me. One night, in a particularly unhappy mood, Anna shouts at me for not scrubbing the linings of the door frames in the fitness centre showers.

But if there's tension over these professional issues, there's even more over who gets paid what. This is an issue which ought to unite us against the management, but sadly it doesn't. Anna knows she should be paid more than the rest of us, because she's the supervisor. Sergio's been promised a pay rise to £4.50 an hour, and Anna clearly regards this as a threat to her authority. Amos knows *he* ought to be paid more because he stands in as supervisor when Anna's not there. Everyone knows they have to look at their payslips carefully to make sure they're getting what they're owed. I'm budgeting for what I think I should be getting paid, adding on extra hours worked as I go along. I'm still waiting for my first payday but the others know what they're getting – and it's never enough. On payday, at around four in the morning, there's a sudden eruption. Sergio, in a fury, storms into the reception and tells me he's resigned. He hasn't been paid for any of his overtime hours, nor has he received his pay rise. (He showed me the letter Marge wrote him about this – four lines threatening dire retribution if he didn't show his deepest gratitude.) Soon Amos is there too, and even the usually phlegmatic Sara.

Amos hasn't been paid for his extra hours, either, and he was owed money for coming in early to clean the offices each night as well. They're all clutching their payslips, and they're all angry. By the end of the night, Sergio has calmed down and decided to stay until he can find something better. But the next day there's a little pile of angry notes to Casna left in the cleaning store. Amos has sealed his carefully in a brown envelope, but Anna has left hers face-up so we can all read it: 'I have noticed you give all the other staff increment on their wages but I didn't receive one. I think if you give increment to everyone I should receive one too. I would be glad if you could pay attention to my request.'

Marge pours oil on troubled waters, promising everyone that their complaints will be dealt with and that if they're owed money it will be paid. But it isn't even clear just what we should be paid. There's a belief that if you do someone else's work as well as your own because of a staff shortage, you'll be paid twice for that – though I never see any evidence of it. Also, the others all say Marge has told them if they work till seven forty-five they have to write on the time sheet that they worked until eight-thirty or they won't be paid any extra. As we've all worked overtime and no one seems to have been paid for anything more than the basic hours, I'm not sure why this belief seems to be so firmly held. I ask for a written explanation of how my pay is calculated, but all I get is a brief, scrawled note from Marge which leaves things little clearer. In the end, I don't wait to find out whether I'll be paid what I'm owed or not – I decide to leave just as my first payday comes around.

Departure

Back in Strathley Road, I've already been making preparations for my departure. I've sent a note to the landlord asking him to use my deposit to cover my last week's rent, and I've told Lily I won't be around much longer. She's been working hard, and when I call in to say goodbye I can see quite a large patch of surprisingly new-looking lino on the hitherto invisible floor. For some reason her mobile phone doesn't take incoming calls but she promises to ring me and let me know how she's getting on. She's as good as her word, and she tells me things are improving gradually. She's found a wonderful woman who can take a huge stack of her books to the charity shop, and the landlord's threats have become less frequent now the smell's receded and the piles of mess on the floor have diminished. A Chinese couple have moved into my eight-foot-square room, she says, and they're very nice. So life is better than it has been for some time. For a while, she continues to phone me from time to time. One night, she rings to say her benefit hasn't arrived, and she has only a couple of pounds in her purse. I pop round and give her £20, telling her she can repay me when she has plenty of money. Of course, I don't really expect her to pay me nor do I really want her to, but she rings several times over the next few weeks to reassure me that she still plans to send the money. Then one night I get a voicemail message saying she's putting it in the post. I don't hear from her again, and I'm afraid it's because she's embarrassed that she hasn't been able to repay me after all. Her phone only makes outgoing calls, for some strange reason, so I can't ring her. By then I've left London, and so we lose touch.

I'm sad about having to leave Lily in Strathley Road, but I'm not even the tiniest bit sorry to be leaving myself. Life here has been a struggle – with the bugs, with the drains, with the poor ventilation which makes the place unbearably airless in summer, probably equally cold in winter. And equally, though I'm sorry to leave my colleagues at the Savoy, I'm deeply relieved to be leaving the job, with its endless tedium and its outbreaks of pointless paranoia.

I wonder whether I should tell my Casna workmates I'm leaving, but in the end I don't. The normal custom is just to disappear. And despite the vain little voice inside me that keeps insisting everyone will wonder where I've gone, I know from experience that within a day I'll be erased from the collective memory, like all the others who come and go, their names merging into one another. The Casna machine will rumble on, as it always does, with a lick and a polish, making do and mending. As I finish dusting the reception for the last time, I take a sideways look at Anna, who is standing uncharacteristically still in the middle of the big entrance hall. When I arrived I admired her slim figure, usually displayed to her advantage in a long pencil skirt and blouse. Just a month or so later her skirt seems to dwarf her and instead of being tucked in neatly her blouse is hanging loose around her hips. The bones in her shoulders can be seen clearly. Not for the first time, I feel a wave of sympathy. Back home, she's someone – her family have a farm as well as a house in town. Here, she's struggling. But somehow – astonishingly, ingeniously, bravely, inspiringly – like countless others across London, she's surviving.

So, is it possible to get by like this in London, on the minimum wage? By the end of my spell here I'm quite sure it isn't. I just about manage to break even on my budget, but only after living for the best part of a week on a single bag of pasta. Then my payslip arrives, and I find I haven't been paid for most of the scheduled extra hours I spent doing offices or for my overtime. I've worked almost 119 hours, not including breaks, and I've been paid £418. My pre-tax pay, over the four weeks I've worked, is just £3.43 per hour. After tax and other deductions, I take home a grand total of £363. My expenses, which consist of rent, transport (I gave up on two-hour bus journeys after the first week and bought a tube pass) and food, come to £474. Even if I'd claimed the £90 housing benefit to which I was entitled, I would still have been £20 adrift. No, I'm sure you can't live on these wages in London. And yet somehow, by staying with relatives or living in hopelessly overcrowded housing, by always walking or catching the bus, by juggling two jobs or even three as well as studying, tens of thousands of people in London do just that.

The final sum:

Hours worked:	118.75
Pre-tax pay:	£418.00
Illicit admin charge:	£10.00
Hourly pre-tax pay	£3.43
Take-home pay:	£363.24
Housing benefit	£89.83
Total income:	£453.07

Spending:

Bedsit:	£260.00
Transport:	£76.90
Food, etc.:	£137.24
Total spending:	£474.14

II

MUPPETS

Seen from the open-plan coffee area here on the first floor, the Frenchgate shopping centre could be anywhere in England. There's a Superdrug, a Carphone Warehouse, places selling trainers and sportswear. This isn't just anywhere, though. This is Doncaster, a town which, like many others in this part of Yorkshire, has always had a strong sense of identity. Or used to, at least, till the pits closed. I used to come here a lot, years ago, because I had university friends who grew up here. Now I'm looking around, wondering what's changed. On a first glance around the town centre, not a lot. Maybe there weren't so many bargain base ment shops in the early '80s, but then again, I might not have noticed. Maybe the concrete of the shopping centre and the multi-storey didn't seem quite so forbidding. But on the outskirts of town I've passed boarded-up shops that would certainly once have done a good trade. On the other hand there are some shiny new metal sculptures in the pedestrianised part of the high street which never used to be here. Essentially, though, it's the same place: its heart hemmed in by too much dual carriageway, its fringes a sprawl of council houses and privately-owned semis.

I'm pretty sure life on the minimum wage here will be easier than my low-pay experiences in London. The capital is by far the most expensive part of the UK, of course, so it should be much cheaper to live in Yorkshire than it was there. The rent will be lower, for a start. I'm expecting to meet different people here, too. The Casna staff were mostly foreign, mostly students, but in this part of York-shire the population is mainly white and indigenous. So I'm expecting my new workmates to have grown up here, to have the support networks of families and friends that the Savoy cleaners often lacked.

I cast my eye over the latest edition of the *Doncaster Free Press*, but the jobs pages look a bit thin. There aren't many positions for people without skills. In fact the only two I can see aren't local at all – they're both in a much more prosperous market town about thirty miles up the road. I ring the first, which turns out to be packing tomatoes in a salad plant. They have just one question for me – do I have my own transport? I say I don't – the minimum wage has just gone up from £3.70 an hour to £4.10, but I still doubt if it would support the running of a car. The second ad looks more hopeful, though: 'Temps R Us are currently recruiting FULL TIME WORKERS for a Multinational Sauce Manufacturer. We offer subsidised transport, cheap factory shop, free work clothing. £4.30/hr + O/T. £175–£185/week. Phone for local interview.' I phone. Again, there's just one question – what's my address? If I'm to get picked up by the factory minibus, I'll have to live on the right side of town. I'll phone back, I say.

I scan the paper again. There are a few flats for around £70 a week, but the only place that will do is a caravan site which offers accommodation for £40 a week. I head out of the shopping mall, navigate the dual carriageway and brace myself for a grey, windy walk across the river bridge. There, behind a pub whose pebble-dash was probably once white but is now stained by traffic fumes and dust, is the grandly-named River View Welcome Home Park. It turns out to be four dingy rows of battered caravans, flanked by a major road and two railway lines. The view of the river, if ever there was one, is obscured by the hulking frame of a new flyover which is under construction about twenty yards away. I meet Bert, the warden, a stout, cheerful fifty some thing with a rolling gait, clad in creased trousers and rolled-up shirt sleeves. As he leads me to the vacant 'van' I'm thinking to myself, well at least it won't have the Strathley Smell, but as he opens the door for me I'm hit by a new aroma – the all-pervasive odour of damp. I'm told later that despite being invisible from here, the river makes its presence known from time to time when it floods out the Welcome Home residents. But still, there's a separate living-room and bedroom, and I have my own kitchen and bathroom too. Despite the smell, it looks clean enough. Someone's made a recent effort to brighten the place up, painting the dado rail in the living-room pink and pairing striped wallpaper below it with flowery above. There's a red dralon sofa, and a little fleur-de-lys pattern on the red carpet. Bert assures me it's quite safe here – there are half a dozen single women living on the site and everyone looks out for each other. I'm not impressed by the flimsy lock on my front door, but I say I'll take it. Bert looks at me, head on one side. 'Are you, er… ?' he asks, quizzically, motioning his head sideways as if indicating something outside the window.

'Er, what?'

'You know, er…'

I don't know. Eventually, he manages to get the words out: 'Are you, er, on benefit?'

No, I say, I'm not. I'm hoping to start a job on Monday. Bert looks mildly disappointed. 'Oh, well, then Yvonne will be wanting cash,' he says. 'Yvonne prefers cash.' I arrange to return in an hour's time to hand over a week's rent plus £40 deposit. Bert doesn't take the rent money, he explains. For that I'll have to see Yvonne, the owner of the site. The deposit's usually £100, Bert says, but without prompting from me he's told Yvonne I can't afford that much at the moment – I can make up the rest later.

As I walk back over the bridge I'm feeling slightly nervous despite Bert's assurances. Who are all these people? In a town where there seems to be plenty of local authority housing, why do they need to live in caravans? Am I going to be living with families who've been kicked out of their council houses? The sort of people characterised by the Home Secretary, David Blunkett, as 'nightmare neighbours'? Still, everyone I've met so far has been perfectly nice. The teenager laboriously polishing his twenty-year-old scarlet saloon car with its customised lamps and spoilers; the elderly woman with Parkinson's, standing by the gate of her neat garden, who smiles and says she's sure I'll be happy here when I introduce myself.

When I return, there's still no sign of Yvonne. I'm not surprised, for Bert has warned me she's hard to pin down. 'A bit of a will'o'the wisp, is our Yvonne,' he said. 'Here, there and everywhere.' I hang around for a while outside the little brick office. In its window is a notice inviting residents to collect money for the 'Children in Need' appeal. After half an hour or so the teenager, who's still polishing his car, trots over to suggest I should ring Yvonne. Alf at number 32 has a phone, he says. Alf at number 32 doesn't look altogether pleased about this suggestion, but he brightens when

I offer to pay. He looks exactly like Uncle Albert from *Only Fools and Horses*, only more nicotine-stained. As he opens the door to his van, which is parked right at the back of the site in the shade of some trees, he apologises for the mess. It's like the very best kind of junk shop in here – rail upon rail of old clothes fill up almost every inch of the dark space, all of them as brown as Alf's beard. There are brown-stained glass cabinets full of brown-stained bone china and cut glass, and by the phone there are brown-stained glass frames cradling sepia photographs of weddings and family groups. There's a saucer of small change – does he save up for the bill this way, or does he just offer a pay-as-you-go service to all the residents, I wonder? On the phone table there's a scrap of paper torn from a lined notebook, with two words written on it in a shaky hand. 'Stop Smocking!' it says. (Lots of people pronounce their 'o's' like this round here. In the factory, later, when a piece of machinery falls apart in my hands, one of my workmates shouts over: 'Ah Fran, yer brock it!') Judging by the evidence, Alf's note to himself hasn't had much effect.

Yvonne promises to be round in ten minutes, so I thank the monosyllabic Alf and head back up to the office. Although he's not a talker, he always gives me a cheery wave and a smile from then on when I pass him in the entrance road, his greasy nicotine-stained cap clamped down firmly and his worn woollen jacket tightly buttoned against the wind. And he's certainly nobody's version of a nightmare neighbour. But then again, neither are any of the other people living here. As it turns out, the majority are pensioners. Why they aren't in council accommodation, I don't know. I barely hear a peep out of them, nor out of the younger people who live here for that matter. There are few families with children, though there are one or two young couples. Some, I guess, may be settled travellers. Yvonne's mum lives here. Bert's already pointed out her 'van', which almost deserves to be called a mobile home, with rendered walls and double-glazed windows. Next to it is a much smaller caravan of the sort which could be towed behind a large car. Eventually, Yvonne, who has a sunbed tan and thick make-up, arrives in a brand new silver BMW of the type driven by city executives. She's wearing a knee-length leather jacket which must have cost several hundred pounds. Her teenage daughter, who's climbing carefully out of the passenger seat, has a full-length sheepskin coat with fur on the collar and cuffs. 'Go and find Grandma,' Yvonne instructs the girl, but Grandma is already limping up the concrete road between the vans on swollen ankles to meet them. This stout old lady makes a strange contrast to these two exotic birds, with her wrinkled stockings and her old crimplene dress. She doesn't come into the office, which has post strewn all over the floor, but waits outside while Yvonne takes my money and gives me a receipt.

Bert helps me to move my stuff in. As he says, it doesn't look much with all the space I've got here. I put my few books and my portable telly on top of the veneered shelf unit in the lounge, but apart from that the only furniture in there is the sofa and a matching pouffe. The bedroom has two white MDF wardrobes but only one of them is usable. The other tends to collapse sideways if I open the door, and the flood water seems to have left the residue of some unspeakable black sludge in its base. Once I've unpacked the place looks reasonably homely, though. Next door to me is Susie. She lives with her elderly mum and five or six fluffy white dogs, each of which sports a little pink bow in its hair. She's been here a long time, she says, and it suits her fine. Her van has its own little garden with a cherry tree and a clematis climbing along the fence. Susie says it's a close-knit community where not much happens without someone noticing, and I can vouch for that. When I call round to introduce myself she already knows my name. Susie is the kind of neighbour who makes a point of popping round to let you know it's bin day tomorrow, or just to make sure you're settling in all right. There are about eighty 'vans' in all, and some of them have exotic names like 'Dominica' or 'Rio Vista III'. Mine is the basic model though, and has 'Mk II Tyne' stamped on the front.

Pickles

I phone Temps R Us again, with my address. They confirm
I can start at Bramwells Sauces on Monday. There's no need
for an interview. The basic pay is minimum wage, £4.10 an
hour, plus 20p extra per hour if I turn up regularly and on
time. I'll work a week in hand and I'll be paid for forty-one
hours a week including five hours overtime at a higher rate.
I should earn about £180 a week before tax. I'll be picked up
by the Shell garage up the road from the site. The driver's
name will be Colin. And so, a few days later, I'm standing on
the main dual carriageway out of town scanning the traffic.
The battered red minibus is only half full when it stops to
pick me up at five to one, but by the time it reaches its des-
tination almost all the places are occupied. I expected most
of the workers to be women, but I was wrong. About half
are lanky lads aged between sixteen and twenty with spots,
short slicked-down hair and tracksuit bottoms. The rest are
an even mix of women, aged between sixteen and fifty, and
older men. At about a quarter to two in the afternoon we
pull into a car park in front of the series of grey sheds with
brightly-coloured trim which is Bramwells. Within what
seems like seconds, everyone on the bus has piled out,
rushed into a hut by the car park, changed their everyday
shoes for work-boots and galumphed off again, leaving me
alone with a plump bloke in his late thirties who tells me his

name is Ken. This is his company, he explains, and in a minute Colin, who drove the minibus, will be along to give me my training and show me around. It's several weeks before I realise that Ken isn't the owner of Bramwells, but of Temps R Us, or possibly of the branch of Temps R Us which seems to run Bramwells' personnel office. I won't be working for Bramwells, he explains. For some purposes I'll be self-employed, for others I'll be employed by Temps R Us. Anyway, I don't need to bother myself with the details because they'll all be sorted out. In the meantime, he sits me down to watch a series of safety videos and asks me to complete a health and safety comprehension test before declaring me clearly 'capable of higher mental processes'. He tells me I'm to be trained up for some special work, along with a couple of other women who started today on the morning shift. In a prosperous market town like this one it's hard to get the age-spread he needs, he explains. Women of a certain … um … maturity, like myself, Sharon and Julie, are especially welcome here. To prove it, he gives me a key for my own locker – a rare privilege for newcomers. I also get a pair of steel toe-capped boots, for which £15 will be deducted from my wages. According to my information the law says employers should provide such safety equipment free of charge. But then again, I'm not an employee. Or am I? I never really get to the bottom of this issue, nor do I find out how being an agency worker affects my rights. I do discover, though, that there are little fleets of minibuses ferrying agency workers all over this area, from the old industrial and mining towns where unemployment is high, to the more prosperous towns where there are labour shortages. Bramwells buses people in from other local towns, including Thorne and Goole, as well as from Doncaster. Whatever the legalities, factories around here seem to find that this casual labour is a useful way of keeping their labour forces flexible.

Soon Colin, who's now wearing a white hard-hat and overalls, arrives to take me over to the main plant. There I'm kitted up with my own white overalls, earplugs, hairnet and cotton cap. He's cheery and friendly: 'If yer need anything, yer just 'ave ter shout: "OI! COLIN!"' he bellows, above the noise of the machinery. Then again, in case I haven't heard: 'OI! COLIN!' Actually, I have heard but I haven't got the knack. It takes me a good couple of weeks to learn to bellow. At first, when I need fresh bottles to stack on to the line, for instance, I'll approach one of the forklift drivers, tug his sleeve politely and trill: 'Excuse me, could I possibly ...' This is not the usual means of communication at Bramwells. Within a fortnight or so, though, I'll be bawling like a trooper: 'BOTTLES!' The 'OI!' is superfluous, I'll soon learn. It's really more a term of endearment than anything else. Surprisingly, I'll find that within a few days I can actually understand what other people are saying to me despite the noise level and the earplugs.

Inside, the cavernous shed-like factory is like a rather cheerful vision of hell. Hulking cauldrons hug their loads of unseen sauces, pickles and ketchups. Bottles jostle one another as they inch into coolers the size of single-decker buses. Huge clouds of steam rise up, denoting unseen processes – filling, labelling, shrink-wrapping. Everywhere is stainless steel. Convoluted arrangements of piping coil back and forth without apparent purpose between bottling lines like the ones you see in films, on which countless jars jangle along at breakneck speed. There's a chest-stopping mix of sauce and pickle in the air. The activity is frenetic. Women pull shrink-wrapped cartons of sauce off the end of the line and stack them on pallets at breakneck speed. Further up the line, the bottles are hurtling out of the la-bellers to be packed neatly, a dozen at a time, into boxes. At one end of the shed, they're packing huge jars of pickled onions, four at once, two in each hand. Most of the machines seem to break down every few minutes, prompting roars of 'JARS!', 'BOXES!', or simply: 'STOP!!'

Colin leaves me in the care of Lara, a pale girl of about twenty with a huge lovebite on her neck. We're sent on our break together. She says she's only been here a week or so herself. She didn't used to work but her fiancé left her a few weeks ago and she's £70 a week rent to pay on a two-bedroom house with a leaky roof. She couldn't understand it, she says. She did everything, all the cooking, cleaning, shopping. Men, she says, world-weary. Can't win with them. Treat 'em mean and they're soppy as hell. Do the right thing and they bugger off without so much as a 'thank you'. Glancing at the lovebite, I say well, with your own place the world's your oyster. 'Yeah,' she says, a bit too brightly. And she laughs.

Tonight we're at the 'stacking end', packing up trays of sausage casserole sauce. Mostly, we're stacking jars on to pallets, or checking for rejects with bad labels or not enough sauce in. Every half an hour or so we swap round, so even the most boring or arduous job isn't too wearing. But we only have two twenty-minute breaks during our nine-hour shift, which finishes at eleven o'clock, and they aren't enough – just time for a quick cup of machine tea, which leaves us thirsty. We're not paid for breaks, of course.

During one of these breaks I sit down with Michael, who's on my line tonight. He's in his early twenties, sharp-eyed and dry. I ask him why are there are such a vast number of different hat-colours and uniforms on display in the factory. There are white hats, green hats, red hats, blue hats, purple hats, even the odd hard-hat. What does it all mean? Michael explains. Women have floppy caps, men have plain ones. Drones wear white caps – all the same for men but pleated for permanent women, elasticated for agency. Quality controllers have green hats, co-ordinators – one down from supervisors – have blue hats and supervisors have red hats. Fitters have purple overalls and purple hats, forklift drivers have green overalls and green hats. Only the shift managers have hard-hats – because, as Michael explains, 'their brains are more valuable than ours'. Everyone wears the same foam earplugs except shift managers, who wear big, industrial-strength headphones. Women have knee-length overalls, men have jumpsuits. Unless they're shift managers, in which case both men and women have knee-length ones. Permanent staff have their names embroidered on to their overalls in green. Some have 'First Aider' embroidered next to their names, in red. I say to Michael, who's an embroidered drone, that it looks to me as if the forklift drivers have the most fun. They swerve gracefully around the factory like ice-dancers on their little green machines, and they have loud, steamer-like hooters to blow if anyone gets in their way. Michael agrees. 'You know how some people dream they can fly?' he says. 'Sometimes I dream I can drive a forklift.'

Of course it's useful in a busy, noisy factory to be able to tell at a glance what each person is meant to be doing. If you need a fitter or a forklift driver in a hurry, it's usually not long before you can spot a blob of purple or green in the distance. But there is something peculiarly English about this need to mark out status. Do we have some inbuilt need to know our precise place in the world – so that we can keep to it, maybe? It's clear those little green embroidered labels have immense significance for some of the Bramwells staff. They show that they've moved up a notch. They aren't at the bottom of the heap any more. But there's something old-fashioned about it, too. It seems to hark back to a world where most people were virtually handed their white caps at birth. It reminds me of that sketch with the two Ronnies and John Cleese, where the working class man wears a flat cap, the middle-class man wears a trilby and the upper-class man has a bowler.

I never fully get to grips with the terms of my employment at Bramwells. One thing I realise early on, though, is that I'm not a factory worker. I'm an agency worker. And there's a big difference. Factory workers get paid more, for one thing. They get paid holidays, pension funds, sick leave. I'm told later by one of the other agency workers that if I stay thirteen weeks I'll probably be offered permanent work with Bramwells. I'm never told that officially, though. Some of the old hands who've been here years tell me they're worried the company may be planning to increase the number of agency workers to cut costs and make it easier to lay people off if necessary. Around here, lots of the factories seem to operate a similar system, and quite a few of the people I meet have worked in several different places, for different agencies. Bramwells has its own personnel office, in the main factory, and one of the Temps R Us staff seems to work for both the factory and the agency.

Learning to fly

When the bus draws up on my second day, there's no sign of Lara. The day after that she's back, though, with a fresh lovebite overlapping the first. She tells me she had to have a day off because her ex-fiancé came round at two in the morning to find out who was in her bed. He's much older than her, she says. He has grown-up kids almost her age. I say well maybe he was worried about the lovebites. Oh no, she says, it's her ex-fiancé who gives her the lovebites.

We spend most of my first week in a department called 'retort'. I ask one of the old hands, Vera, what this means and she says she hasn't a clue. What she does know, though, is that one of the major supermarkets had this extension built on to the main shed so we could make extra specially creamy sauces. They come down a long chute from the main factory, from precisely where I never find out. Then they're packed into an enormous oven and when they come out again they're cooled, washed, wiped (by us) labelled, packed (us again), shrink-wrapped, and stacked (this is the worst job because the shrink-wrapping is still hot and sticky when you lift the cartons, and it burns your hands if you're not quick about it.) There are packing labels for each carton, which in some parts of the factory are put on by machine but which here must be put on by someone standing next to the shrink-wrapping machine: slap, slap, slap.

The most exciting job, and the most difficult, is packing. The veterans make it look so easy, but to me and the other newcomers it's a mysterious black art. It's a bit like learning to fly, I decide. At the start, you just flap about hopelessly, trying to fit your eight bottles into your box and count off eight for the next packer before your own next eight come along. But it's all happening too quickly, and you've barely got off the ground at all before you've crashed, and bottles are spinning all around you, plummeting off the end of the line, smashing on the floor beside you, being swept off the line on to any bit of spare space by agitated workmates. Sooner or later, though, and it could happen suddenly and without warning, you will find yourself airborne. It's the best feeling. All at once, instead of fighting the machine, dreading its next move, you're part of it, and the two of you are gliding along together. The tiniest thing leads to another crash, of course – the feeling that someone's watching, or a loud noise from nearby. But as time goes on and you manage it time after time, you begin to wonder how you ever found it so difficult. Now you soar along, popping your eight bottles nonchalantly into their box and then relaxing while you wait for the next batch to trundle down the line.

Even at the plummeting stage, though, everyone's behind you. The first time I get off the ground, concentrating furiously on what I'm doing, I gradually become conscious of Colin standing behind me with Vera. I can almost hear them saying, 'Go on girl! You can do it!' Of course, I crash. But not before my fraught performance has raised a little cheer of encouragement from my workmates. I have time, as I flail around trying to recover myself, to reflect that one could profitably paraphrase Dickens on this subject – production line moving one millisecond slower than packer: result, perfect harmony. Production line moving one millisecond faster than packer: result: total chaos.

What I really want, of course, is to get up to the cooking department to find out what goes into those jars of cook-in sauce and ketchup. But it doesn't happen. That's a whole different section, I'm told. Shelley, a cheerful bleached-blonde Brummie who flirts indiscriminately with all the lanky lads, says she's been here three months and she's never even been up the filling end, let alone into cooking. So I have to content myself with reading the ingredients labels on the bottles. 'What are we packing?' I ask Shelley one day as the first trolley-load of a batch of unlabelled sauces trundles down the chute. 'Oh, it's that Coma Sauce,' she responds with a knowing look. 'It's an own-brand for one of the supermarkets.' We've just been packing own-brand 'Coma Sauce' for one of the other supermarkets, so I ask whether there's a difference. 'Oh yes,' Shelley assures me. 'This batch has to have the labels stuck on just right, or we have to reject it.' I soon realise this response is not due to some congenital stupidity on Shelley's part, but to the culture in the factory. The fact that we're packing familiar foodstuffs is somehow set aside. We're not dealing with pickles and sauces, but with 'product'. What goes into the bottles is really no concern of ours unless it's too runny or the wrong colour, or there isn't enough of it. While the new-comers peer at the labels, wanting to know where every-thing's going, what's in it and how much it will cost, the veterans just want to know how many bottles to a box, and in what pattern the cartons should be stacked on to the pallets to ensure they don't collapse when the forklift man comes.

Carnage

Sometimes, though, the nature of the product is hard to ignore. Towards the end of my first week, I'm sent up to pickles for the day. There seems to be some sort of problem, and they're short-staffed. When I get there, I can see immediately what's wrong – there's been a pickled cabbage explosion of gigantic proportions. There are piles of red cabbage everywhere. The production line can barely be seen for glistening, steaming mess and purple ooze. Every little ledge and cranny on the elaborately-laid out filling machinery is concealed by the stuff. The workers look like participants in some avant-garde art installation, their white overalls splattered with abstract purple shapes. And as for the floor, earth-moving equipment is surely going to be required if it's to be seen again today. No one seems too fazed, though. Someone gives me a rubber broom and a shovel and I set to work alongside all the others to clean up. Once the shovelling is done, the hosepipes appear. And surprisingly quickly, the place is beginning to look itself again.

I'm helping Jane, the co-ordinator, who tells me she's been working here fifteen years: 'I left once, but I was so bored I came back after a few weeks.' As we pause for breath, I ask her what went wrong with the last batch of pickle. She looks at me strangely. 'Oh, nothing,' she replies. 'It just gets like that when you're doing cabbage.' As it turns out, beetroot isn't much better. By the end of the night the place looks as if it's been witness to a bloodbath again. I have several jobs during the day – the simplest involves standing at the huge round plastic filling table, pushing beetroot through round holes in its perimeter into bottles below. The most mind-numbing job, and the messiest, involves sitting on a stool by the production line as 300 open jars of beetroot hustle past every minute, poking my fingers into each one to ensure the 'product' isn't poking over the top when the lid goes on. I'm allowed rubber gloves – I need two of course because I must use both hands and still perform two or three well-aimed jabs per second to keep up with the line. But this doesn't protect the rest of me from the waves of beetroot and vinegar which fly out of the jars and off the sides of the line, landing like little bursts of hail in my lap. From time to time I brush it off, but with little effect. Soon I'm covered in purple blotches, like everyone else.

Standing at the filling table Jane and I fall into wondering at the quantities of beetroot which go through here each day. 'I often think about it,' Jane says ruminatively. 'I mean, where does it all bloody go?' I start doing a few calculations. This line – one of two permanently assigned to pickled cabbage, beetroot and onions – runs for seventeen hours a day Monday to Thursday and thirteen hours on Fridays when we work a short shift. That means roughly one and a half million jars of pickle leave the line each week. On the day I'm there, we turn out beetroot for eight hours solid – 150,000 bottles, and that's just one batch for one supermarket. And we can't, I'm sure, be the only pickle factory in the country. I begin to wonder idly whether we are in fact fuelling some vast EU pickle mountain. Maybe the truth is more prosaic – maybe we're just gearing up for the Christmas rush. It had better be a busy one, I decide. At the end of the shift Jane tells me I've done OK. 'If you come again,' she says helpfully, 'you should ask for a floor-length rubber apron from the clothing store.' Thanks, Jane, I reply silently.

Our conversation sets me thinking about pickles. Is there something inherently funny about them, I wonder? Do they have some sort of inbuilt Alan Bennett-esque Northern humour about them? You only have to say the words 'bottled beetroot', or worse, 'economy grade pickled cabbage', to summon up a smirk. One of my fellow minibus travellers tells me he's been here two months but his mates down the pub still howl with laughter every time they see him. 'Yer a pickle packer!' he yells in imitation. ''Ow many packs of pickles did yer pack today?' I think maybe it's just the futility of it all. I mean, who needs pickled onions? The answer to that question, as I've already calculated, is, 'Plenty of people'. The economy's sliding, the world is at war and all around is doom and gloom. But Bramwells is working overtime – I've even been asked to come in on Saturday to help fulfil the demand. The old hands don't see anything funny about it, though. They seem to have become inured. One night during my first week I go up to the canteen in the midst of a minor production crisis and announce without thinking: 'They're in a right pickle down there.' Then, realising what I've said, I laugh and add: 'Well, I suppose they would be.' Blank stares. I feel under pressure to explain myself. 'Erm. Pickle factory?' I flounder. Then the penny drops, and everyone starts to laugh.

Swear

Mind you, there's nothing humourless about the workers here. It's a bit like that Victoria Wood sitcom, *Dinner Ladies*, with added F-words. But though the white coats and floppy white caps give that impression, and there's plenty of laughter, the sitcom characters are far more self-consciously respectable. 'Fran,' Jane announces to me mock-serious as we sweep our beetroot into the jars, with a nod to a huge fan behind us: 'I want you to know that blower's going right up my arse.' It's not unusual to hear one stout fifty-something remark to another, as they embark on their third or fourth pallet of jars, 'Ee, Vera, I'm *fucked*'' It isn't something people learn after they arrive at Bramwells, though. Julie and her friend Sharon started the same day as me, and they've barely got their feet under the production line before they're swearing at the other workers like troopers. By day three, Julie is giving it the full four barrels because one of the permanent workers has told her she's not putting the caps on the brown sauce bottles fast enough. She says she's being slowed down by a defective cap-twizzer. 'If 'e says one more thing to me,' she growls menacingly, 'I'm gonna *twat* 'im one. E's got me right wound up. I'm 'avin a right stressful day, and 'e's just standing there like a cunt wi'is flamin' arms folded. I don't know if I'm comin' or fuckin' goin'. And,' she finishes with a flourish, 'now I'm 'avin one of me 'ot flushes as well!'

I'd put Julie down as being in her early fifties, but in fact she's forty-four. I have this problem with a lot of the other workers here. I don't know if it's the effect of smoking and heavy drinking, or whether it's due to stress. Julie must have been married by her early twenties. Her oldest son's twenty-three now. She's separated from her husband and she's bringing up her teenage daughter on her own. She used to be a nurse, but the stress got to her and she decided to do something which wouldn't take so much out of her. Mind you, it doesn't seem to be working. On the day of the cap-twizzing incident, she gets so wound up she has to go to the pub for a calming drink when she finishes at three, and it takes her till midnight to get calm enough to go home. She won't be defeated by a mere hangover, though. She's back and clocking on as usual at five to six the next morning.

Nothing stops Julie working. During our second week she strains her shoulder stacking cartons, and within a day or two it's so inflamed you can see the lump through her overalls. The factory nurse sends her to the local hospital for a check-up, where she's told to rest. And does she? Does she 'eckerslike, as they say round here. She's back on the production line within an hour, and though the supervisor puts her on labelling to prevent her making it worse, she's still rigid with pain. From time to time she gets angry because something needs lifting and no one's doing it, so she does it herself. Then she has to turn away, biting her lip and hiding her face from the rest of us so we can't see how she's suffering. She really, really wants to hold on to this job, she says. If she takes time off she'll lose pay. But what worries her even more is that Temps R Us will think she's a slacker and then she'll be sacked.

Sharon, who I'd assumed was about the same age as me – thirty-eight – turns out to be a mere twenty-six. Mind you, that may have had something to do with a conversation we had on one of our first shifts together. Sharon told me she lived with her fiancé, who worked in another local factory – they'd been together five years, and they were planning to get married next year. Her mum had despaired of her ever getting married, she said. It seems twenty-six is old, around here, to still be unmarried. Sharon lives down the road and she says Bramwells used to have a bad reputation – a few years back, its agency workers were paid about £2 an hour. Things definitely seem to have improved recently, she says. Her brother works upstairs on the cooking shift, which starts at one in the morning. It's mostly powder and stuff, she tells me.

Colin, the shift manager who doubles up as a minibus

driver, is concerned enough to come round several times over the next couple of days, to see if Julie is OK. She isn't, of course, but she always says she is. It's extraordinary, though, how that shift-manager's hard-hat changes Colin's personality. In the factory, he's caring, warm, low-key (relatively) and always polite. Put him in front of a steering-wheel, though, and he's a different man. All the way home, he keeps up a stream of abuse so mellifluous it's almost an art form. Like many people round here, he doesn't speak in sentences. He simply strings all his syllables together into a single word, pausing only to slip in the occasional glottal stop or, just once in a while, to draw breath. 'Mo*vo*wweryer-foreyetwat! Yercd'v*gorrableeedin'tank*inthier!' he will scream as we roar up to a junction. Or 'Chuffin'*ecky*edaf-cow! Gerroutathafuckin'way willyer?' Then he'll stop to pick up a passenger and suddenly he'll be wearing his caring manager's face again. 'Hey, Lara baby! How're ya doin? Everythin' OK?'

As well as conducting these sixty-mile round bus trips each day and putting in a nine hour shift in the factory, Colin works as a bouncer at weekends in the centre of town. How he copes, I don't know. But he says he's got two houses to keep – he bought his council house then moved to another place. Now he lets out the council house.

Colin is the only person allowed to smoke on the bus. He went to Mexico for his holidays this year, he tells us, and he had to have one of those nicotine inhalers to get him through the flight.

Almost all the workers, both in the factory and on the bus, are white. But on my bus there's a middle-aged Asian guy, Ahmed, who sits at the back and doesn't say much while the youngsters swear and banter together. Ahmed tells me he's only been there a couple of weeks but he's already thinking of leaving. He's been put on to pickles, which makes his chest sore. But worse than that, he's just had his first pay slip. The company pays £4.30 an hour, but Ahmed hadn't realised he'd only be paid that if he turned up on time every day. On his first Friday he missed the bus and he was late – so he only got £4.10 an hour for the whole of his first week. Ahmed has three sons, all of them at college, but he worries about them. They should be working as well as studying, he feels. They're not making enough of a contribution to the household budget. 'Well when I was at college, I had to work as well,' Ahmed tells me. 'I don't see why they shouldn't do the same.' He's done a book-keeping course at the local college, and he manages to get some book-keeping work which he does in his spare time to supplement his wages. He also has a flat that he rents out, but he says it's more trouble than it's worth. There are always arguments about the rent, and who should pay the electricity bill.

I'm deeply relieved Ahmed isn't on the bus the day its

passengers get on to the subject of race relations. The Americans are bombing Afghanistan, and though it hasn't been a major issue for discussion it does come up one night. Wayne sums up the prevailing view, to approving nods, murmurs and cackles from the assembled crowd. 'We're definitely anti-Taliban here,' he announces. 'But that's just because we 'ate all fuckin' rag'eds.' Just once or twice, I see Ahmed's culture clashing painfully with that of the rest of the passengers. 'You know that woman you're bringing in for a shift tomorrow, Ahmed?' Colin asks one night. 'Can she speak English?' Ahmed says no, she can't. Then Colin laughs. 'Is she single?' he chortles. In the darkness at the back of the van, I can feel Ahmed wince. He doesn't reply.

The Al and Dave show

Colin drives the bus on the afternoon shift. And though he may lapse occasionally into crassness, the morning bus-driver, Duncan, makes him look like Noel Coward. I meet Duncan for the first time at five in the morning on the Monday of my second week. I'm on early shift, and I've been told I'll be picked up at the garage as usual. As I pull back the rickety sliding door of the van, I can see a little wiry man in his mid-thirties wearing a dirty white baseball cap. He's hunched over the wheel as if he's at the starting line of a Grand Prix. I'm the first passenger on the bus, and Dunc doesn't say much until we stop at a former pit village down the road and his mate Dave gets on. Dave swings into the front passenger seat: 'Good weekend, Dunc?' Then it starts. 'Worrafuckin'weekend! Fuckin' game on, mate!' As we hurtle down the main road towards the factory at seventy miles an hour, gaily ignoring those light-up signs in the thirty zones that say 'SLOW DOWN! KILL YOUR SPEED!', the story of Dunc's weekend is embroidered into ever more fantastic patterns. By the time we reach the factory he's been with four different women since Friday, concluding his last encounter about an hour before he picked me up. He's discovered a really great joke, which involves ringing up various women he knows, with his mates, at two in the morning singing that Barry Manilow song from the BT ad down the mobile phone at them. You know the one, where the guy wakes up in the morning and his wife plays back a phone message to him, and it's him and a crowd of other blokes singing 'I LURVE YOU, *BABY* …' This has tickled Dunc so much that he can't get it out of his head. I've been assigned to his line, and throughout the day I can hear little bursts of the song drifting up from the stacking end. In fact this refrain continues for a full two weeks, during which time I learn a great deal more than I really need to know about the anatomies of Dunc's various girlfriends. Secretly, I wonder if Dunc really spends his weekends shopping with the wife and kids. Then, in one of his more serious moments, he tells me it's a year since his wife left him. Things start to fall into place after that. Now he lives with his teenage son, and the two of them often go off clubbing and drinking together. They get on brilliant, he says. He had a fortnight off in the summer and spent the whole time in an alcoholic blur. Before he came to Bramwells he used to work for the council as a van-driver.

Although Dunc's boisterous nature marks him out, his fondness for the drink certainly isn't regarded as unusual. 'Fuckin' drank ev'rything me, Sat'dy,' one teenage girl tells her mate on the bus one Monday morning. 'Fuckin' tequila slammers, the lot. You name it, I drunk it. Fuckin' soaked, awas.' For many of the workers here, certainly the unattached ones, life seems to consist mainly of five days at the factory and four nights on the piss, with the occasional footie match on the telly thrown in. On Friday afternoon, the volume on the bus radio is pumped up. Kylie Minogue is always there, singing: 'Lalala, Lala Lalala,' endlessly. Everyone's planning the night ahead, talking about where they'll go, who they'll meet, what they'll drink. Friday, Saturday and Sunday nights are definite drinking nights. Monday is a little more doubtful. It depends on how much cash there is left after the weekend. Furtively, little plastic bags of cash are pulled from pockets on the journey home. 'Drop us off at the Bay 'Orse. 'I've still gorrenough for a pint,' Dave will tell Dunc with some satisfaction after a quick cash-check. Tuesday, Wednesday and Thursday tend to be quieter nights, of necessity. Hangovers are regarded as a sort of occupational hazard: 'Well it wor gwinter be a shed,' Dunc explains puzzlingly one morning. 'Mightus well mek it a large shed. A garage, even.'

Dave is scarcely any different – if anything, he embroiders his tales even more fancifully, as if trying to re-create himself in Dunc's image. One Monday, he tells us he and his girlfriend went out on Friday night, got drunk and swapped underwear in the Chinese takeaway while waiting for their chicken chow mein to arrive. 'Right down to me skin, I was. Everyone was watching us, even the Chinkies,' he explains with faint surprise, as if it were normal custom under such circumstances for the owners of the take-away to avert their eyes. I'm almost inclined to believe this tale – I mean, why bother making it up? I'm less convinced, though, that Dave's girlfriend is really paying for a weekend trip to Amsterdam so she can watch him having sex with a black prostitute. But then again, who knows?

Dave, it turns out, is a master of self-reinvention. I'm shocked when I discover we're the same age, for he's had so many reincarnations that I'd assumed he was a young-looking late forty-something. This comes of necessity rather than choice, though. Dave left school at sixteen and did what most young lads in this area used to do back then – he went down the pit. It provided a good living and, so far as he knew, a job for life. He got married, survived a year on strike, got divorced and remarried, then agreed to take re-dundancy because he was told it would save the pit. A year later the pit closed anyway, and the people who'd stopped on all got an extra £7,000 redundancy. (Dave still talks about the strike as if it was yesterday. 'I learned to cook nettle soup during the strike,' he'll say, knowing everyone will know immediately which strike despite the passing of sixteen years and much change.) I suppose Dave is typical of many people round here. After the pit closed, his second marriage broke up. He worked in another pit for a bit, then in Germany, trying to find a way of matching the £30,000 salary he'd lost. He's had the compo, of course. About £28,000 – nearly a year's salary after giving up fifteen years of his life, along with the health of several of his body-parts. He's got vibration white finger (£8,000), industrial deafness (£2,000) and asthma, even though he doesn't smoke. He hasn't had anything for that. He seems to have learned to take what life throws at him, though. He's back living with his mum now, in her council house which he's bought on a small mortgage. On his days off, when he's not in the pub or swapping underwear in take-aways, he's cutting down some trees in the garden and putting in a new driveway. That's only recent, though – he was living with a girlfriend until a few weeks ago, someone much posher than him. 'She wanted to take me round to all these parties with her mates. I just felt like a piece of meat.'

Dave comes to sit with me sometimes at break in the canteen. He's clocked me for someone with an education, though I've never said anything to suggest it. I think it's the fact that I read the *Daily Mirror* while I'm eating my sandwiches. I've started buying it because the only papers left lying around in there are the *Daily Sport*, the *Daily Star*, and if you're really lucky the *Sun*. 'You're always reading, you. Always got your nose in that paper. Mind you, I like to keep up with stuff myself,' he tells me. 'I used to read the *Guardian* at one time.' As I say, Dave has learned the art of reincarnation. At the moment, I think he's wondering which way to go next. He says he's happy enough, mind you. He's done agency work in a few different factories recently. He's got a bit of money so he can get a woman when he wants one and sleep alone when he wants, he says. If he wants a day off, he can always take one – unpaid, of course. He goes to the pub when he chooses – cash permitting – and goes home when he chooses. Just occasionally, though, the sense of what he's lost creeps through. One day, I'm packing salad cream into boxes with Duncan on my right and Dave on my left. We're taking it in turns to sing songs to pass the time. Dave has contributed 'Halfway up the stairs', in a falsetto, Kermit-style warble, and insists I should take my turn. So I lead the way in a rendition of the Muppets' theme tune, with me doing the 'Me *ne* mer ner' bits, and Dave and Dunc filling in with the 'Do *doo* do do-do' parts. Dave laughs and says to Dunc: 'It didn't take long to turn *her* into a muppet, did it?' I say I'm not sure I want to be a muppet. Dave's smile fades as he pauses for a moment, deciding whether to explain. 'Fran,' he says eventually, '*All* agency workers are muppets.'

Underclass

It's true, there's a deep divide between us and the permanent workers. Although they're friendly enough they're also conscious of their higher status, and I think some of the older ones regard us with a tinge of suspicion. After all, we're paid less than they are. Once or twice, I hear people voicing the fear that Bramwells might take on more agency staff in order to get rid of permanent employees.

I'm now on a regular team, made up of a mixture of Bramwells and Temps R Us staff. Usually we're on catering sized ketchup – 'TK', as it's known in the trade – or sometimes on smaller-sized bottles for supermarkets. Up at the filling and labelling end there's usually me, Sharon and Julie, stacking the bottles on to the conveyor, wiping smears and putting on the caps. Down the bottom end, packing and stacking, there's Dave, Duncan and Wayne, all agency staff. Then there's Liz, the quality controller, Tim, John and Alison, who are regulars, and the supervisor, Phil, a polite man who seems, unusually, to get by without raising his voice. Tim likes to climb on the machinery to fix ketchup pipes in place or deal with mechanical problems. John – the cause of Julie's wrath over the cap-twizzer – seems to spend most of his time standing with his arms folded. Alison deals with the messier mishaps, which are about the only interesting thing that really ever happens on 'Catering TK'. I'll be minding my own business, getting into the rhythm, learning to lift three of the empty ten-pound canisters on to the conveyor at once, then four. Then suddenly there'll be a slurp from the filling machine and Alison will be extracting a mangled mess of plastic and gunge from its innards. Then the hosepipe comes out, then the wet-wipes. It's easy to cause chaos – not only by working too slowly, but also by working too fast. Give the bottles a little shove to help them down the line, and they start piling into the labelling machine too fast, then there are sticky bits of paper everywhere, all with 'Chef's Kitchen' printed prettily over a little green ladle logo. Or alternatively you can turn a single carton the wrong way – handle pointing backwards instead of forwards, and there's that slurping noise again.

I haven't seen Lara, my companion on my first shift, for a week or two. (After she doesn't appear for a few days, the minibus stops one afternoon at her picking-up point – Colin says she's been ill but has promised to return today – but there's no sign of her and her answering machine is on. 'Waste of bleedin' space,' Colin mutters as he revvs up the van.) But one day she reappears, trotting into the portable office as I'm picking up my pay slip. I'm surprised to see her: 'I thought you'd left.' She looks equally surprised, as if not being at work for a couple of weeks and not phoning in when she's not coming are quite usual, in her world. She explains, mildly hurt, that she's been ill every day for the past week and a half, except Saturday and Sunday, when she felt better. Today she overslept, but Ken from Temps R Us came out to pick her up in his car. It's the end of the early shift, so we go for a cup of tea. I ask if her fiancé has come back yet and she says no, he's still living with his new girlfriend but he visits regularly to check up on her. She wouldn't be working at all if he were there, she tells me. He used to pay all the bills. Now she's starting to worry because she's going to have to sign off soon, and then she'll have to find all the rent by herself. I look at her, a bit shocked. 'You're still signing on? You've been working for weeks! Lara, you'll get done!' She says yes, she's been thinking that. Maybe she'll just sign on one last time this week and then she'll stop. 'I'm going to have to start coming to work every day aren't I?' she asks, as if she's hoping I might have a better suggestion. She seems so innocent, somehow, as if life simply hasn't taught her these simple mechanisms for getting by. She reminds me of a girl I once knew who'd spent most of her life in care – both vulnerable and trusting at once. I've only known her a week or two, and she's telling me stuff that could get her into serious trouble; asking my advice as if I'm some kind of a mother figure.

But Lara has other things on her mind today. She shouldn't have been here actually, she tells me. She was supposed to be at a meeting with the social workers about her kids, but she 'bottled it'. Kids? How old is this girl? She's twenty-one, she tells me, and she has three of them. Not from her most recent fiancé, with whom she's spent the last two years, but with her previous boyfriend, with whom she spent the previous five years. By the time she was nineteen she already had a daughter and two sons. They were taken into care two years ago after it turned out her boyfriend had been hitting them. She says she didn't know about it, and she's been fighting ever since to get them back, but now she's been told they're going to be adopted. 'I'm an unfit mother,' she says matter-of-factly. 'I can never have another baby, because if I do they'll take it away.' I ask if she wants another. She thinks for a moment and says yes, she'd like a girl – 'So I've had two girls and two boys.' She looks sad for a minute but then she brightens. 'Hey, me and my ex-fiancé went to Bridlington for the day on Saturday,' she says. 'It was great.' They'd got there early but it was cold so they went into an amusement arcade. They spent £60 on one of those grabber machines and she won three fluffy toys. Then they had a walk about, had some dinner and went into another arcade, where she spent £20 on the slot machines. Then they bought a piece of rock shaped like a penis as a present for her friend (that cost £7) and went home again. Her ex paid for the lot.

Lara really hasn't got the hang of working. She simply doesn't have the concentration to stand on a production line packing sauces all day long. She'll arrive at work, get dressed in her overalls and boots and go to whichever line she's been assigned to for the day. But within an hour or two she's twitching. She simply can't stay. She wanders off to the office to talk to Colin, who knows every detail of her love-life, she says. Or she'll ask to go to the toilet and then call into the nurse's room to say she's ill. She's never worked before because she's always had money from the social or from her fiancé. I suppose in some respects she fits the irresponsible teenage mum cliché. But she's never had a council house, and the private one she does live in has holes in the roof so she has to put pans under them to stop the drips. And if she was clever, she wouldn't be coming to work at all. If she just signed on and didn't work she'd get her rent paid, plus £45 a week benefit, which is a lot more than she's taking home from Bramwells at the moment on the hours she's putting in. One way or another her benefit is going to stop soon, and if she can't gather the skills she needs to come to work every day and on time, she's going to lose her house because she won't be able to pay the rent. I know I should be disapproving of Lara. She's not typical of the workers I've met here. Look at Julie, soldiering on with her swollen shoulder. Even Duncan always turns up and works hard all day without complaining. But she's pathetic, like an open receptacle waiting for anything that might fall on her. Children, relationships, they've just happened. If she was ever going to make anything of her life, she needed to be taught a few basic survival skills a long time before now. If she'd had parents who'd taken her to school every morning and picked her up every evening, for example, wouldn't she be more capable than she is of doing the work she now has to do?

Lara is surprised to hear that I was in the office picking up my payslip – she's not bothered to collect hers, let alone to check whether she's been paid what she's earned. I look at mine – for the second week running I've been short-changed. I worked a week in hand so last week, my second week, I was paid for my first week. But somehow, the office staff managed to pay me for four days instead of five. By the time they'd deducted my £12 bus fare and the £15 I had to pay for my safety boots, I was left with £120 gross – a long way short of the £185 mentioned on the job ad in the local paper. I took home £106 after working a forty-one hour week. Looking at my second week's pay, I find that I've been repaid the day I'm owed, but now two hours' overtime pay has been dropped from my second week. So this time I'm £11 short. When I protest again, I receive an envelope with £7.50 in it, which is enough for two hours at the basic rate of £4.30, minus tax, rather than the higher rate I should be paid for overtime. I give up. I've done enough complaining. Later, my third week's pay is a further £11 short. I calculate that if I'd done as many of my colleagues do and simply pocketed my pay without checking it, I would have received £3.85 before deductions for each hour I worked in my first three weeks. And that, of course, doesn't take into account the £15 the company should have paid, according to my reading of the law, for my boots. Factor that expense in, and the hourly rate for my first three weeks drops to £3.73. Still, to my amazement I find I haven't come close to spending my wages. The cheap rent and reasonably-priced transport has left me dramatically better off than I was in London.

The razz

I'm left wondering how my workmates manage to have such active social lives, if they're taking home so little money. Many of them will only get £4.10 an hour because they've arrived late or taken a day off sick without phoning to let the company know in advance. Some of them have other incomes, of course — one of the women works in an off-licence three nights a week. She finishes there at about eleven o'clock and she's back on the production line at six. Colin has his nights as a bouncer. Duncan gets an extra tenner a day for driving the bus, and he saves a further £12 a week because he doesn't have to pay the bus fare. Some people live with their parents, others have council houses, so their rent is comparatively low. Dave tells me he gets £45 a month compensation for the drop in earnings he's suffered since the pit closed. It doesn't come close to making up the difference, but it does cover the mortgage he took out when he bought his mum's council house. So, he says, the money he takes home from here is really just to cover his beer, his take-aways and his weekends in Amsterdam. Mind you, he's a bit smarter at budgeting than I am. One day, he's showing me with mock pride the collection of little sticky labels he's peeled off his dinnertime fruit, each one neatly stuck on to his sandwich box. I jokingly tell him he's a bit short on brand loyalty – he's eating Coxes one day, Granny Smiths the next. I stick rigidly to the West Indian bananas I buy in the super-market. Dave looks at me witheringly. When you go to the market on a Saturday afternoon, he tells me, you don't argue about whether you're getting an Orange Pippin or a Victoria Plum, you just take what's cheapest and smile nicely in the hope that the stallholder will throw in an extra one.

Some of my workmates have given up better-paid jobs to come here – Julie was a nurse, Sharon had an admin job in an office. Both of them found the stress too much. Now they both want jobs they can go home and forget, and they're planning to stay on long-term at Bramwells if they can. For others, though, Bramwells work is easy-come, easy-go work. Some of the younger agency workers are just there making a few quid so they can enjoy Christmas. After that, they'll look for something else or sign on again. Every day, as the battered minibus travels along its route, there's someone who isn't at their appointed place along the way. After my second week I don't see Ahmed again. I suspect Lara won't last much longer. Even Duncan, who seems like a veteran, has only been here a couple of months. He just wants enough for his mortgage, his ale and his women, he says: 'Me shaggin' allowance.'

I feel I should experience the local nightlife. After all, it's a central feature of life around here, and it seems to have its own, quite unambiguous flavour: if it gets you pissed quickly and cheaply, it'll do. There's an ad running at the moment on the local radio for some kind of party night in a club, which seems to sum it up perfectly. It's sponsored by an obscure brand of vodka. 'Blue Parrot Vodka,' runs the pay-off line, 'Just Drink It.' Not: 'Blue Parrot – a taste of the exotic,' or even 'Blue Parrot – because you know you're a gorgeous bird.' Just Drink It. Gerrit down yer neck.

I've been meaning to look up an old friend who lives in Doncaster, in any case. She suggests we meet up on Friday night in a bar on the high street – one of the more up-market drinking spots, and also one of the quieter ones. When I get there at eight o'clock it's already heaving, and the speakers are pumping out music with a heavy beat. It's one of those stripped-wood places, and strong German beers cost about £2.50 a pint. Boddington's is just £1.30, though. After one glance around the room, I can see why Duncan turns up for work every Monday morning with his 'tash full of glitter. Nights out round here are glittery kinds of affairs. Glittery trousers, glittery navel-rings, glittery transfers that you stick on your bare shoulder so it looks like there's an S-shaped line of diamonds stuck to you. My friend's told me to expect a certain amount of flesh, and it's here, protruding from bra-tops, halter-tops, hot-pants, mini-skirts. There are even trousers you can unzip all the way up the sides so everyone can have a flash of your knickers. This isn't just for the young, svelte women, either. There are all shapes, sizes and ages here, and outside the window they're tottering cheerfully from bar to bar in great waves, in a sort of community crawl that gives the town centre a carnival air. Winter has arrived early and there was snow in the air this morning, but there isn't a single coat or jacket in sight. I'm wearing a cardigan and a jacket and I feel cold just watching. For the men, the uniform is a neatly-pressed baggy shirt over proper trousers with the creases carefully ironed in down the front and back. Proper shoes, nicely polished, not trainers. Everyone's made an effort. Hair is carefully lacquered, women's nails elaborately painted. Friday night is clearly something of an event. There's no denim at all – it's banned from many of the bars, along with trainers. My friend was refused entry to one place last week because she was wearing a denim skirt – though if she'd had the nerve to take it off in the street and go in wearing just her knickers, there wouldn't have been a problem. In some places the rule only applies after ten o'clock, so if you're in by five to, there's no problem. They won't throw you out, once you're in, unless you start a fight.

We finish our beers and set off down the street. There are bouncers on all the doors, but we don't pass the club where Colin works. You don't really need to go to a club, as it happens, because lots of the bars have two o'clock licences so you can carry on drinking without paying an entrance fee. One of these bars is our next port of call – a vodka bar which feels more like a nightclub. It can't be later than nine o'clock, but inside here it's dark and the music is so loud it feels as if it's coming from inside you. There's a certain amount of glass and chrome, and though it's too crowded to tell whether there's an actual dance floor or not, people are already dancing. There's a menu with a staggering range of vodkas on offer – you can even get chilli-flavoured vodka, if you really want to, but I'm told the local drink of choice is vodka and Red Bull. A jug of this evil brew costs ten pounds and contains ten shots of vodka. The Red Bull has caffeine in so it keeps you buzzing, and it's served in this way in almost all the bars. At the next table, a group of women are drinking it straight from the jug, passing it round from one to the other. We order a jug, with some glasses. It's sickly sweet and it tastes a bit like Vimto – you'd never guess it had alcohol in. In what seems like no time at all we're out on the street again, heading for a slightly alternative pub where there's less glitter, some of the lads have Beatle haircuts and there's Bob Marley on the jukebox. Alternative it may be, but it still sells jugs of vodka and Red Bull. We order another one. Then some beers. Some time later, I find myself falling out of a taxi at the door of my caravan. I still have change out of fifteen pounds in my purse. On Monday I ask Sharon if they drink vodka and Red Bull round her way, too. She confirms they do, and tells me she and her mates were drinking it with vanilla liqueur chasers the other night. They leave their jackets at home, too – it's a style thing, but it's also useful because if you take a coat you're bound to lose it sooner or later in the rush from pub to pub. That's just Friday night, of course. On Saturdays, you go out with your boyfriend or husband and then you usually wrap up warm.

Nemesis

The demise of Duncan is almost Shakespearean in its in-evitability. There's no sign of the van when I get to the petrol station on Monday morning and when it finally arrives, a quarter of an hour late, I'm inside phoning Temps R Us. Duncan looks a little more tense than usual as he clenches the wheel. What kind of weekend has he had, I ask as I climb aboard. Despite his lateness and his beleaguered air, I'm hoping he'll perk up and start into his usual cata-logue of conquests. But he doesn't. 'Don't talk to me about it, he says. 'I took bird number one out on Friday night, took 'er back to my place and while I was in the bog having a Jimmy Riddle she read all the text messages on me mobile phone. One on'em says, "D'yer fancy a shag?" Another says, "Missing you already." She went ballistic. I thought it weren't too bad 'cos I were thinking of binnin' 'er anyway. Then she rings up the other three and tells 'em I'm shaggin' 'er as well as them. Only the married one's still goin' ter see us.' So poor Duncan is down from four girlfriends to one (married) overnight. He's spent the rest of the weekend drowning his sorrows, it seems. I tell him unsympatheti-cally that I would have done exactly what 'bird number one' did. 'Yeah, well yer a woman,' he replies. There's no malice in his voice, just resignation.

There's worse to come. As we blare along the main road

ignoring the 'Slow Down' signs as usual, we spot a police squad car in a turning. Duncan brakes sharply but it's too late – the police car pulls out and follows us. About half a mile before we get to the factory, the blue flashing lights come on. Duncan stops and gets out. Two other police cars pull up behind us. Dave is in the front, watching Duncan through the wing mirror and narrating: 'They're giving him a ticket,' he says. Then, 'They're breathalysing him.' A minute or two later, the driver's door opens and a female officer pokes her head in: 'Can any of you drive this van?' We all shake our heads mutely. None of us want to get involved. 'Your driver is being arrested,' the policewoman goes on. I ask what for, and she pauses before replying: 'For failing a roadside breath test.' Duncan, it turns out later, has more than twice the legal alcohol limit in his blood. It's a good job they didn't give him a bullshit test too, I reflect – he's told me more than once that he never drinks when he's driving the van the next morning. We all watch as Duncan is bundled into the back of the police van and locked into a cage inside, his off-white cap still crammed down over his ears. I don't expect to see him again – after all, how many firms would keep on a driver who gets arrested for drink driving in the company van with passengers aboard?

Bramwells would, it seems. About lunchtime, like Banquo's ghost, Duncan appears at the bottom end of the production line – he was able to walk here from the police station once they let him go. We've all been talking about him in the past tense for the last six hours, so the apparition comes as something of a shock. His demeanour doesn't help, either – he's a shadow of his usual rumbustious, chanting, cackling self. Dave gives him a hug and says, 'It could happen to the best of us, mate.' I could swear I hear Wayne saying under his breath, 'No it couldn't,' but I might be wrong. No one's prepared to criticise Duncan to his face. The general consensus is the police were out of order. It was entrapment, Duncan says to murmurs of agreement. The police made right tossers of themselves, bringing in all those reinforcements just for him. Anyway, if you're only twice over the limit you can ask for a retest. He should have done that. He has to see Ken, the Temps R Us boss, tomorrow – he's away today – but his deputy's told him he doesn't think there'll be a problem about his job. He'll have to stop driving the van, of course, because he's in court in a couple of days and he's bound to lose his licence. Duncan plans to clock off for a couple of hours, go to court then come straight back to work afterwards. I won't be there to hear the verdict, because I've decided to leave – an announcement which makes few ripples, given the excitement over the arrest.

Moving on

Saying goodbye to the River View Welcome Home Park is easy. I have never, ever, been so cold as I've been living here. The bed was so damp when I moved in that on my first night I slept with a hot water bottle and had to keep lifting the duvet to let the steam out. Gradually it dried out, but it never got any warmer. In a metal caravan with no insulation you're only warm if you're sitting on top of the electric radiator, and the meter uses up about £5 worth of electricity if you leave it on overnight. As well as my duvet and hot water bottle I've acquired first a woollen blanket, which I double up, then a borrowed second duvet. Sometimes I put a cardigan over the top of them but it still doesn't prevent me from waking up in the night shivering. And you know how people talk about beds and sofas being so old that the springs are poking out of them? I thought that was just a turn of phrase until I slept here. Having a bath is a shivery and laborious affair, too. I have to put the immersion on a couple of hours in advance, then try to be in and out of the bath in about five minutes flat. Any longer than that without clothes on in this atmosphere is more than I can take. In any case the bath is only half-sized, so my legs poke out over the taps and the overall experience isn't a particularly therapeutic one. On the plus side my lack of a fridge is not a major problem, for the milk lasts several days in my cold kitchen without being refrigerated. And having my own space is a real luxury. Not having to share the bathroom, as I did in London, is liberating and it's good to have a whole kitchen to rattle around in after living in one tiny room. There are no bugs that I can see, either. They've probably fled somewhere warmer.

It's turned out to be a quiet enough little backwater, if a grimy and cold one. It's tucked away behind a major road junction, and if you didn't know it was here you'd never stumble upon it by mistake. I'd expected to be disturbed by other people's music at the weekends, at least – after all, the walls are so thin you can hear a flea cough three vans down. But apart from the sound of the trains, and the construction workers during the day, I don't get disturbed much at all. My neighbour Susie pops round occasionally to make sure I'm OK. Both her daughters have just had babies, and she's glowing with pride. 'Mum's waited eighty years to be a Great Grandma, and now she's become one twice in a month,' she tells me. Susie works in a pub, and drives to and from her job in an old Saab which is kept on the road by Jim, down the bottom, who is 'brilliant and very cheap'. If I need a car he can get me a good one for about £300, she tells me. When I drop my mobile phone getting out of my van in the dark one morning, she lends me hers so I can ring it up to see whether I can hear it. I can't though, and I never see my phone again.

I don't even see most of the neighbours, though. After all, I leave for work before daylight and return as it's getting dark, and it isn't the weather for lounging around outdoors. Bert says I'm not the only one with a full-time job. There's a man who works in an office in Nottingham. Commutes every day – got a flat there but moved back within a week. He couldn't stand it. It was noisy, for one thing. And there's a woman who works in Hull, though she's decided she has to move because with winter coming on the travelling is getting a bit much for her. Bert acknowledges there's a social stigma about living in a caravan, though. One man moved here after his wife had thrown him out, but she turned up after a few days and took him back. 'She said she couldn't have her old man living in a bleedin' caravan,' Bert tells me. At work, a few people are curious about the idea of living in a place like this, though others are familiar with the concept. Dave tells me there are quite a few similar caravan parks in the area, and Lara says one of her friends lived in River View for a bit. One of the other workers said she thought it was 'a gypsy site', though. Sharon wanted to know if there was a shower block, like you get when you go to Rhyl on holiday. Others envisaged something rather grander than the reality, with all sorts of things laid on, like a shop and a laundry. It could have been worse, but then again a house or a flat would be a hell of a lot better. As I drop my keys through Bert's letter box, I don't suffer a single of pang of regret.

And so I bid farewell to Bramwells. How have I been treated? With more humanity than I was in London, certainly, though some of the same problems have recurred – having to pay for my own safety equipment, in particular, and the regular under-payments. But I find that in a friendly, co-operative atmosphere, my resentment about these things is considerably less. You can look at it two ways, I suppose – a smile and the odd kind word costs nothing, and if it means workers are less likely to complain when they're not treated well, then it's worth the effort. I don't think Bramwells's attitude is that cynical, though. Sure, there are two classes of people here – the permanent staff and the agency 'muppets', as Dave brands them. And it's often the agency people who do most of the donkey work of stacking, filling and packing while the permanent staff are on hand to deal with problems. But the presence of a number of decent, caring managers like Colin and like Ken lifts the whole atmosphere in the factory.

Despite the underpayments, getting by on the minimum wage in Yorkshire has been much easier than it was in London. I always earned my extra 20p an hour for punctuality, which helped, and the hours were better than at Casna. In London I applied for a job which looked as if it was forty hours a week, but ended up being paid for only thirty hours although I worked more. In Yorkshire, I worked forty-one hours a week and on the odd occasion that I got the right money in my pay packet, five of those were overtime hours paid at time and a third. My rent was just £40 a week instead of the £65 I paid in London, and my bus fare was £12 compared to the £22 I had to pay in London. The temptations are fewer, too. I rarely find myself popping into a café here for a cup of tea and a piece of cake, not least because I'm working longer hours and have less leisure time.

I won't miss the mind-numbing boredom of the work, but it's not without a slight sense of regret that I take my leave of my colleagues. Colin holds my hand and tells me I can come back any time. Julie gives me a hug and wishes me good luck. Duncan doesn't say anything – he just keeps on working away quietly. When the line stops because of some glitch and everyone gathers to chat, he stays separate, leaning forward over a stack of cardboard sheets, looking away from the group. It seems unnaturally quiet today despite the roar of the factory. I find I almost miss his singing, drifting down the line. On the bus home, one of the managers drives and Duncan sleeps all the way.

Hours worked:	140
Pre-tax pay:	£552.15
Deduction for safety boots:	£15.00
Final pre-tax pay, before complaints:	£537.15
Hourly rate:	£3.83
After complaints:	£582.43
Take-home pay:	£492.53

Spending

Bus fare (sometimes under-charged)	£33.00
Rent:	£160.00
Food, etc.:	£141.73
Total spending:	£334.73

III

WHO CARES?

Autumn has given way to winter now and there's little to relieve the dark landscape as I travel further north, into Scotland. I've picked out a town near Aberdeen, a neat, buttoned-up, well-to-do place where oil-fuelled affluence keeps the supply of minimum-wage labour short. There's a sparse gentility about the place that puts me in mind of a Scottish comedian I once heard describing childhood visits to a well-heeled but rather mean auntie: 'You'll have had yourn *tea*?' she would remark hopefully as she opened the front door. Everything here is clean, respectable and turned in on itself. The windows of the big grey houses might as well all be tightly shuttered for all the warmth and humanity they radiate. Some are set back in their own gardens, gloomily self-contained, but the solid terraces on the main streets feel cold as I walk by, too. Even the Christmas lights twinkling prematurely along the high street do little to lighten the tone.

I'm looking for a job as a care assistant, something that's advertised at £4.10 an hour or thereabouts in almost every local paper in Britain. This place is no exception. With a sizeable elderly population and whole streets of impressive Victorian houses just crying out to be turned into nursing homes, it's clearly a fertile hunting ground. I'm a little concerned, though, that finding work will be more difficult in my latest chosen field than in the previous ones. After all, I'll be caring for some deeply vulnerable people. Surely there'll be questions about my background, demands that I should demonstrate some relevant experience? It's not so, though. When I phone the Towers Nursing Home to arrange an interview I'm told I'll need a couple of referees, but if one of them can vouch for me on the telephone I should be able to start work in a couple of days.

And so I set off through the town's affluent outskirts, where the heavy terraces give way to imposing detached houses. From its name I'm not expecting the Towers to be a cosy place, and from the outside it isn't. Perhaps its builder found the plain, solid architectural style of the neighbouring houses too stern, perhaps he hoped the mock-medieval turrets and huge, studded oak doors would add a touch of grandeur. Whatever the aim, the effect now is merely to make the place look even more forbidding. I hear later that the house was abandoned for years. The doors are locked and the bell rings hollowly inside, failing to evoke a response. Eventually I walk round the back and find the kitchen door wide open. Inside, there's a warm, steamy atmosphere and a soupy smell which drifts out behind me into the oak-panelled hallway. Along with the dog-eared carpets, it creates a surprisingly homely air. In the lounge a dozen or so residents are sitting motionless in their armchairs, and next door in the dining-room a few are equally inert at the tables. One woman is inclined slightly forward over an abandoned cereal bowl, a dewdrop distending from her nose.

Tina, the matron, turns out to be a blowzy woman of about fifty who talks incessantly and only asks for the barest details about me. She asks if I have any experience, but seems unconcerned when I say I haven't. She'll give me a three-day induction, she says. By the end of that I'll know whether I'm going to like it or not. There are about thirty residents in the home, most of them classed as 'very frail'. Most staff do either days or nights, and days are split into 'earlies' and 'lates' – seven till two or two till nine. I should come in on Monday for an early, and then we'll see where we can go from there. The pay is £4.10 an hour on weekdays, £4.40 at the weekend with an extra ten pence an hour 'attendance' money if I turn up regularly and on time. There are two fifteen-minute breaks for which I won't be paid, so the hours add up to thirty-two and a half per week. I can get extra shifts if I need them, though. Pay day is monthly and I've just missed one, so I won't be paid for four weeks. This stream of information takes a while to deliver as it's constantly interrupted by the ringing of the phone and by Tina breaking off to talk to a man of about sixty who keeps popping his head round the door to ask: 'When are we gan' oot?' 'I'll take you out later if you're good!' she hoots at him, louder than she needs. 'But you have to be good!' A minute later she's scolding him for asking again and as I leave, by the front door this time, she's pushing him back into the hallway. 'You've been bad. You won't give me a minute's peace! No, we won't be going out today!' I suspect, rightly as it turns out, that this ritual continues unabated throughout each day. Tina promises to phone me once she's spoken to my character referee, to confirm that the job's mine. Later she'll send out tick-box forms asking if I'm honest and reliable. I've asked a couple of friends to vouch for me and this turns out to be perfectly acceptable. I'm told later that the phone call is a brief one – just a formality, Tina says.

Fast food joint

The search for accommodation turns out to be a bumpier ride. My first scan of the local paper yields virtually nothing apart from an agent offering 'letting rooms' from around

£200 a month, all of which have gone when I phone. One-bedroomed flats are way out of my price range at around £400 a month and upwards, and bedsits don't even seem to exist around here. I don't see any ads for mobile home sites, either, though even if there was one I'd be reluctant to take it. The weather's getting colder by the day and I can't face the thought of any more sleepless nights in a freezing, damp bed. I look at a room in a shared house which is surprisingly neat and situated very conveniently in the middle of town, but it's being let by an agent who demands a minimum six-month lease and threatens to withhold my deposit if I leave sooner.

So what do people do around here if they don't qualify for a council house and they can't afford to pay market rents? Eventually, I find out. I decide I may have to resort to a down-market bed and breakfast, and answer an ad in the paper which says: 'Hotel. Good area. Fr. £60 per week, £12 per day.' Caledonian Lodge turns out not to be a hotel at all, but what can best be described as a sort of hall of residence for people with jobs. It's a peeling 1960s block divided into corridors with about eight rooms and a shared kitchen on each. Some, including the one I'm shown, have their own bathrooms and cost £70 a week. On top of that I'm told I'll have to pay £7 a week for electricity and hot water. I'm overjoyed – this means I can have all the showers I want, and I can leave the heating on all night if I feel like it without having to pay extra. The building's grubby and threadbare, but the room's reasonably neat. It's about twelve feet square with built-in white MDF wardrobes and even a couple of shaky bedside units to match. There's a double bed with a rather thin, overwashed duvet and the bathroom has a slightly grubby shower cubicle. The walls are off-white and bear the marks of previous tenants' blu-tac and drawing pins. I know I'll struggle to pay the rent but it feels like luxury. In the kitchen there's a fridge and freezer, even a quite new microwave. There's a room with a washer and dryer which cost £5 a load to run, so I'll no longer have to spend hours each week sitting in a launderette. The place seems to be managed by its owner, who shows me around, and his wife. I guess there must be about fifty rooms in all. I'm told it hasn't been refurbished for a while because there's talk of redeveloping the site. They don't take benefit claimants and there are hardly any students. Almost everyone is working. As I unpack my belongings I run some rough calculations through my head. I reckon I should take home about £130 a week, which leaves £53 a week after I've paid the rent. As it turns out, Caledonian Lodge is only about ten minutes' walk from the Towers and quite close to the shops. That means I'll be able to walk everywhere, so I won't have to pay transport costs. I'll have to buy my own uniform for work, though, a tunic which I'll need to wear with black trousers. The tunics cost £18 each and I'll need two, but I've been told I can wear my own trousers and a T-shirt until I get paid.

I venture into the kitchen to heat up a pizza. Someone's wedged open the window with a jar of mango chutney, presumably to let out cooking fumes. It's freezing in here. A quick glance at the grill pan and the inside of the oven reveals why this is necessary. There's a thick layer of blackened grease, probably built up through years of casual use and even more casual cleaning, which must fill the place with smoke the minute the cooker's turned on. I'm wondering whether to attempt a full-scale cleaning exercise or just live with it when the door opens and a middle-aged man comes in. He introduces himself as Jack, and when I tell him I'm about to start work at the Towers he knows immediately where I mean. 'Ah', he says. 'The haunted house.' He's a taxi driver so he sometimes picks up 'the girls' from there at the end of a shift. They seem to like it well enough, he says, with a hint of hesitation in his voice. I assume at first that Jack must have recently arrived here from somewhere else, but he tells me he was born and bred locally. He's worked away, he says, in the North of England and in Glasgow, but he's been back and living in Caledonian Lodge for almost a year. It suits him fine, he says. Where else could you find somewhere so warm and so cosy and so *convenient* to live for £70 a week? His car, an old Peugeot, is parked outside with a variety of others, most of which are about ten years old. One has a ladder on the top and belongs to a window cleaner who lives downstairs, Jack tells me. Some of the people here are just passing through, or work locally but have family homes elsewhere. But in the main, they just live here. Single blokes, or ones who've been divorced and can't afford anything grander. As I put my pizza box in the bin I notice there's already a 'Beef Dinner with Dumplings' in there. Tonight Jack is having a 'Steak and Chip Meal'. Later, I come to recognise these as the staple fare of the Mace store on the corner of the street. They also do 'Mince and Tatties', or for a change, 'Haggis and Tatties', for about £3 a go. I get the impression this is an almost entirely male billet. The grease on the cooker, as it turns out, doesn't present too much of a problem because it's largely been abandoned in favour of the microwave.

The Towers

Such is my pleasure in my thermostatically controlled convection heater that I turn it up too far and awake in the night with the unfamiliar feeling of being uncomfortably hot. I have a lie-in, too, after weeks of four-thirty starts to catch the Bramwells' minibus. Now, with my shift starting at seven, I can get up at six-fifteen, have time for a shower and a cup of tea and still be at work five minutes early. Even after I arrive at the Towers, there's a relaxed start to the day. I'm shown where the kettle is, and then for twenty minutes or so half a dozen of us sit in the lobby listening to a monologue from Tina about her weekend. She's being stalked, she says, by her former deputy, desperate to get his old job back: 'So I told him, which part of N-O is it you don't understand?' She repeats this more than once, to polite laughter. Meanwhile the overnight staff nurse runs through a roll-call of the residents: 'Lizzie, no problems; Maud, no problems; Maggie, fine; Rose called down in the night to say she had diarrhoea. Well, what do you expect? She did have two dinners ...' One of the residents, Margie, has a sore knee, which is causing some consternation because her son has asked for the GP to be called. The intrusion is clearly unwelcome. There's a great deal of tutting and sighing, especially as the family have 'persisted in taking her out' yesterday despite everything. Later, though, I hear that she's to be sent for an X-ray, 'to satisfy the relatives'.

I'm handed over to Carol, a trim, sensible 'senior carer' of about forty-five, who's to show me the ropes. Today, she says, I can just watch her. Tomorrow, she'll watch me and then after that I'll be on my own. We have about half a dozen residents to rouse, wash and breakfast before we have our own break at nine thirty. The building is three storeys high and it soon becomes clear that the higher up you go, the poorer the residents are. On the ground floor, all the rooms are single-occupant and have their own bathrooms. On the first, some are single and some are shared but most have only a sink and no toilet. On the top floor are big rooms with low, sloping ceilings, most of them shared by three residents with one sink between them. Up here, the chests of drawers are often half empty and if you pull out a pair of pants, likely as not it'll have holes in. Most of the residents, I'm told, are paid for by the local authority. Only a few can afford the £500 a week, or thereabouts, that the Towers charges in fees.

Most of the residents wear incontinence pads, but Carol tells me I must check carefully to see if they *really* need changing. She introduces me to a new and yet important concept in the carers' vocabulary – nappy abuse. One of her daily jobs is to count the pads in each resident's cupboard to make sure it tallies with the number in the 'toileting folder', where we're supposed to record each change. In the front of this folder, Tina has stuck a fifteen-page notice in bold type about the need for everyone to desist from changing residents when they don't need changing. (These pads are clearly a major expense. Later a friend who does shifts in lots of different homes tells me that she went to one where they had to change an incontinent resident's sheets every hour at night because it wasn't deemed necessary to provide them at all.) Carol tells me if I do need to change someone's pad I should use a wipe and foam from an aerosol to clean them. There are surgical gloves in most of the bedrooms but she doesn't use them for this job, nor does she suggest I should. She teaches me how to lift wheelchair-bound residents from bed to chair, and back again, one hand under the armpit, the other under the thighs. 'You should be trained to do this but I'll just show you for now,' she tells me. And that, as far as lifting goes, *is* my training. Later, looking at the residents' care plans, I realise many of them are supposed to be lifted using a mechanical hoist. This is meant to be better both for them and for us, but it doesn't happen. Several of the carers have bad backs. I suspect if they complained they'd be told they should have stuck to the care plans.

When I tell Carol how much I'm paying for my accommodation she suggests I put my name down for a council flat. Hers has two bedrooms and costs £137 a month, she says. She's grateful for it because her husband's had an accident and he can't work so they have to live on her wages. This takes them just above the benefits threshold, apparently, so they're not entitled to any top-ups. I've been told most people on these wages locally will be in council accommodation, but when Carol introduces me to today's morning shift, they turn out to be a pretty mixed bunch. Shirley has a council house, which she shares with her partner Dave. They have five children between them. Dave works at the Towers, too. Apart from him, though, there aren't many male staff. It's the only place I've worked where women are definitely in the majority. There's Elsa, who comes from Nigeria, and Gail who comes from Australia. They're both married, both living in private rented places. Sally is younger, hoping to train to become a nurse, and she lives with a boyfriend who runs his own business. Lisa, a gutsy twenty-year-old bleached blonde, has just moved into a rented flat by herself.

The dance

There's a rhythm to the day here that didn't exist at Bramwells. In the factory there was no distinct pattern, just bottles hurtling by all day long. Sometimes we'd even stop mid-batch, when our shift finished and another team came to take over. But here, there's a proper rising and falling. The home is like a great beast breathing gently. In with the morning, out with the afternoon. Days of the week, months, seasons, make little difference. The comings and goings of visitors, with their aura of chilly fresh air, are but transient things. Flies that land on the creature's great flank, soon gone.

When I arrive at seven, the building's a sleepy place though not a sleeping one. The night shift are putting their coats on, one or two residents are up and wandering in their dressing-gowns: 'What do I do now?' 'I want the toilet.' Soon someone or other will steer them back into their rooms, plonk them on a commode, start rifling through drawers for decent underwear. The best part of my day's work will be crammed into the next two hours. I soon fall into a pattern. First breakfast on a tray for Maud, in her single room on the ground floor. Maud likes to do everything for herself but her arthritis is bad and she's slow. If you pause outside her door you can sometimes hear her, berating herself: '*Why* have you got odd stockings on, Maud? Because you're stupid, Maud, that's why.' Then upstairs to Ella, a tiny bird-like woman who's bed-bound after a stroke. When she opens her eyes I put on my cheerful voice, designed to sway her mood. '*Good* morning Ella! How are you today?' It doesn't work. Most queer, she says. Her husband came in earlier than usual last night. It was quite inconsiderate. Oh, dear. Ella is having one of her mornings. As usual, she's quiet while I change her pad but from then on our routine is punctuated by questions: Is her bad arm hanging down? Are her legs touching each other? Are there enough pillows under her legs? No, no and yes, Ella. Do I know she can't take her yellow pill till she's had her red one? Yes, Ella. I fetch Gail to help me lift her into her chair, put her breakfast in front of her and heave a sigh of relief as I pull her door to behind me.

Down the corridor, Lizzie is lying awake but placid. She

doesn't speak, just gives me one of her looks. It's a friendly sort of a look. When I ask how she is, she says: 'Am arright.' Her accent is much thicker than Ella's. While Ella is bone china, translucent, Lizzie is reddened and broken-veined. As usual, she's been put to bed with her teeth and hearing aid in. She hates taking her teeth out. If you push her, she'll gag on them till she's sick – something she does with spectacular ease. Once Lizzie's dentures are cleaned and re-inserted, it'll all be plain sailing. Clothes on, into the wheelchair, downstairs for breakfast. Upstairs again to help Ella back into bed. She wants Drapolene cream on her bad arm, she says. Drapolene is nappy rash cream and she doesn't have a rash. But it seems to be used here as a cure-all for troublesome residents, so I give her some. I don't suppose it will harm her. Yes, Ella, your covers are on in the right order. No Ella, you won't fall off the bed.

Then back downstairs to Rose. Rose can do some things for herself, if you give her a bit of encouragement. She's just confused. Some days, she's miserable and whispers over and over, 'Oh, I don't like this. I don't like it at all.' But today she's cheerful. When I ask how she is, she says fervently: 'Oh, *much* better.' She's puzzled when I pull down the duvet, though, for there's a bandage on her leg. 'What's that?' she asks, the first of several times. 'Don't you remember? You cut your leg.' 'Oh,' she says. There's a colour picture of a young woman in a graduation gown, but Rose can't remember who she is. She's pretty sure the black and white picture of a girl in nurse's uniform is her, though. 'Oh this is super!' she keeps saying. 'Super Dooper!' I steer her through to the dining-room and take a sideways glance at Freddie, breakfasting quietly with his girlfriend Marion. Freddie, who's in his late seventies, has his own room on the ground floor but usually sleeps upstairs with Marion. He can do most things for himself but I have to check he changes his clothes every day. Today they look clean so I decide to leave him be. A little later I'll encounter him and Marion in the corridor, Marion struggling along on her bad knees, Freddie following behind with her handbag. They both smile a lot but they don't say much. Lila is already up and dressed, too. Her clothes are the ones she had on yesterday, but she's added a hat made of a commode shell. It's painted bright green on the outside and has a pink flower stuck to it. I catch her and coax her back upstairs to the room she shares with Violet and Ida, to change.

Already it's time for break and I haven't tidied the bedrooms yet. I'll have to catch up later, as usual. We make sausage sandwiches from the residents' leftovers and eat them perched on rows of institutional, wooden-armed chairs in the dark, narrow staffroom. The notice board is crammed with Tina's bold-print notices: 'Owing to an incident in which a visitor allowed a resident to go out, the combination code for the front door is now PRIVATE and must not be given to ANYONE. Breaches of this rule will be treated as a DISCIPLINARY OFFENCE.' 'It has come to the attention of management that certain staff are not paying for their meals. Please note that in future staff without vouchers WILL NOT RECEIVE FOOD. Costs are: Main meal, 50p. Soup or pudding, 20p.' No one ever asks me to pay for my sausage sandwich, though. When we emerge, the lounge is subsiding into torpor even though residents are still parked higgledy-piggledy in their wheelchairs, like a motorway pile-up. Once they've been lifted into armchairs the place looks neater. Janie, one of the more able residents and ever the optimist, has already handed round the chocolate biscuits in anticipation of a cup of tea. Lizzie has smeared hers down her dress. Violet has licked the chocolate off hers, and it's all round her mouth. I start shovelling sugar into teacups while Shirley pours, instructing: 'Three sugars for Martha … four sugars for Lila, no milk for Marion. Don't let Emily have any sugar, she's not allowed.'

Tea done, cups retrieved, it's nearly time for lunchtime toileting. The worst job of the day. Back into the wheelchairs again. I'm 'pulling down', today, removing pants and pads while Lisa and Margaret hold each resident in mid-air. Martha is soaking wet, but as usual there's a chorus of 'Ach, it's just tea …' The residents of the Towers have a remarkable ability to spill tea down the backs of their dresses while seated, it seems. Such an accident does not demand a change of clothes. Anyway, whatever sort of liquid it is we don't find it all that offensive. Alice, though, is a different story. Today she's dirty. She's been sitting in it, of course, and as she's flopped on to the toilet it smears all over her leg and the seat. I use five wipes to get her clean, while the others watch. 'This young lady,' Margaret says to the air, 'Is afu' partic'lar.' I'm not sure whether she's referring to Alice, or to me. We wheel everyone back into the dining-room for lunch. It's half-past eleven. Today it's Tuesday, so it's cold roast lamb, marbled with fat, with mashed potatoes, carrots and gravy. Half of it goes in the bin, as usual. Violet, who has deep lines on her face and a kindly expression, has been confined to her chair in the lounge. She's got that look that says she might throw something, Tina says. Mind you, she's sitting placidly enough, one hand resting casually in her pink blancmange pudding.

Sometimes, maybe about once a week, a man will arrive after lunch with an accordion to play 'Daisy, Daisy,' and 'The Mountains of Mourne'. When this happens, we all dance. Freddie is in demand because he's the only male, and he bustles off to change into his patent leather shoes. Marion looks on, smiling indulgently as he takes a turn round the room with half a dozen female residents. Emily tuts as she guides me carefully around the floor – didn't anyone ever teach this girl to waltz? Some of the residents sleep through the performance or stare into space, but others come to life when they hear the old tunes. Even Ella, alone up in her room, is humming along to 'Flower of Scotland' when I take her tea up.

There are other, perhaps less welcome, forms of entertainment. One Sunday the doorbell rings several times in quick succession and each time I open it there's a group of fresh-faced, middle-aged visitors in tweeds and capes standing on the step. I'm surprised, for there are rarely more than a few visits from relatives in a single day. It isn't long before everything becomes clear, though. These people are here to conduct a religious service. Emily is delighted – she was a regular church-goer in her time, and misses it. But when I ask Margie if she wants to sit nearer so she can join in, she replies with an emphatic: 'No. I do *not*.' This is the only time I really encounter religion during my time in Scotland. In London, one of the very first things my African workmates wanted to know was whether I went to church, but both here and in Yorkshire it seems mainly to be confined to weddings and funerals. Even among this elderly population, Christianity doesn't seem to be of central importance to most people.

There are other visitors, too, though there are fewer of them than I'd expected. I'd say that in the month or so I spend here, the majority of the residents have no friends or family to see them at all. Some have letters or postcards from abroad or from other parts of the country; Freddie receives a large box of chocolates from a nephew. Ida's daughter comes almost every day and sits with her, and Margie's husband comes in with *her* daughter a couple of times a week. But some of them don't seem to know what to say when they do come. They sit round the one of the tables in the dining-room, looking at a familiar face and knowing the mind behind it has left them. That this person with whom they spent much of their life doesn't really know who they are. No wonder some of them keep their visits short or don't come at all. Most of the residents barely even notice. But there are some for whom it matters. While I'm at the Towers, one inmate has her seventieth birthday. The doorbell rings just as we're serving lunch, but when I offer to keep her meal warm her son – I presume – says there's no need. Within five minutes, he's handed over a scrappy bunch of flowers and a card and he's gone again. As she sits down to lunch, there's disappointment written across her face.

Once the post-lunch visitors have departed, everything goes into reverse. The doorbell ringing as the late shift arrives. Late shift is just like morning shift, backwards. More tea. More toileting. Supper, about four-thirty. More torpor. More toileting. Television, a late-night snack at about seven. Then the residents go quietly, one by one, to bed. By nine, the beast is semi-comatose again.

I soon realise this job, much more than cleaning or

factory work, has both light and shade. The good moments are great, the bad ones horrible. Some of the worst moments come when the residents are upset and out of sorts. Sometimes, this is predictable. Bathtime is often a flashpoint, for example. No one wants to be bathed, and many of the residents resent it deeply. One night, after I've given Ida a bath, she cries for half an hour while Shirley holds her hand and tries to comfort her. Other times, there doesn't seem to be any particular reason for it. Sometimes Alice won't eat her lunch, for example. When I try to coax her one day, she throws it at me then starts hitting me so hard she leaves little bruises all over my arms. Then there are bodily fluids, of course. I'm told I'll get used to them, but I don't. Sometimes Violet eats her own excrement in the night and when we arrive in the morning it's dried on to her teeth and in her hair. It takes Carol and Shirley two hours to clean her up – I'm spared that for now, because I'm new.

But day after day, I'll emerge nauseous from lunchtime toileting to an encounter which more than compensates. I'll go to find Margie to bring her to lunch, and she'll fling her arms around my neck in an expression of pure, unalloyed joy. 'Och darrrlin' I *love* yer!' she'll cry, as if overcome by gratitude for some act of kindness. 'I do love yer!' Sometimes there'll be tears in her eyes. Or Rose will be standing in the corridor looking lost, and I'll take her arm. 'Oh, I'm so lucky to have you. So lucky …' she'll breathe, overwhelmed by her gratitude. Neither of them can remember my name, of course. But it makes no odds. Every encounter is a brand new adventure.

I suppose the unique element of this job is its human relationships. Old age and institutionalisation have worn away the residents' inhibitions as well as their memories, so friendships are quickly formed, quarrels quickly forgotten. When the short-term past is a blur, you tend to vent your frustrations on the person who's standing nearest to you. But equally, when you can't remember the name of your husband or your daughter you're just as likely to offer your undying affection to the stranger who happens to be putting your stockings on for you today. In this job, there can be real delight in going to work.

Dreaming

There are more practical reasons for choosing care work, too. Take Shirley, for example. She's a comfortable, motherly soul in her early thirties. She used to work as a cleaner, but in this job she can do what she's best at, which is caring for people. And the shifts allow her to see the kids at least once a day, before they go off to school or when they come home in the afternoon. It isn't easy, though. Shirley does days, and Dave does nights. He looks after the youngest ones in the daytime while Shirley's at work. That means they barely see each other except on their days off. It also means they have to snatch a few hours' sleep whenever they can. One day, Shirley's late for work. She tells me she slept in because her little girl was wide awake at one in the morning – Dave let her sleep too long during the day because he needed the rest himself.

I'm in awe of Dave and Shirley. How on earth do they get by on what they earn with five children, I wonder? They have a car in which Dave drops Shirley off if she's on a late shift, but she can't drive and if she's on an early she has to get a taxi to work. If she's on a late, she has to get a taxi home. Their council house is on the other side of town, and it costs her £7 a time. The only alternative is three buses. With the early starts and the late finishes, she just can't do it. The fifteen-year-old has to babysit while they're changing over shifts and she doesn't like to leave him with the responsibility for any longer than she has to. She tries to get a lift with one of the other carers when she can, but as often as not she can't. She earns £28 a day and as often as not a quarter of it goes on taxis. I work out she and Dave take home about £15 a week more than they'd get if they were on benefits. And if they *were* on benefits they wouldn't have to pay Shirley's taxi fares or the kids' school meals. A cynic might say they shouldn't have had all those kids. But it's easily done. When they met, Dave already had his two boys from his first marriage living with him. Shirley had a little girl from an earlier relationship. Then they had two more together. If she was a doctor and he was a solicitor, no one would bat an eyelid. I don't find out until later that they should be entitled to about £80 a week top-up benefit – Working Families Tax Credit so I never get a chance to ask them whether they claim it or not.

One day at break, Shirley pushes her hand into the pocket of her tunic and pulls out a small brown envelope. Her expression says she's thinking of doing something she shouldn't. 'I'm just wondering whether I should post this off or not,' she says. It turns out to be one of those ads credit companies send out in the post. Shirley already has £1,500 on her existing credit card and she's up to her limit. Christmas is coming up, and with all those presents to buy she can't really see much of an alternative to going further into debt. She's determined she'll clear it by next summer, though, because she and Dave are getting married and they both want the wedding to be really, really special. They're having the full works. Big dress. Three bridesmaids. A matron of honour. A pageboy. One of the biggest churches in town. Reception at one of the best hotels, £16 a head. Evening buffet, £5 a head. Photographs and a video, £600. Two stretch limousines, another £600. The stretch limos are Dave's big thing, apparently. He's been down to see them, and they're the business. They even have a drinks cabinet and a video player in them. The glass is smoked so you can see out, but other people can't see in.

A couple of days later, Shirley comes in with a bit of good news. Her dad has offered to pay for her reception. He can afford it, she says. He has a good job as a lorry driver. He goes on holidays, so she knows he has plenty of spare cash. She wouldn't take it, otherwise. With that covered, Shirley and Dave will have to pay £5,000 for everything else. Shirley's planning to work 'doubles' from January to July to earn some extra money. My heart goes out to her – it all seems so hopeless, somehow, so certain to lead to even more hardship. She's going to be exhausted before the wedding, and even such a gargantuan effort can't do more than take the edge off the level of debt she'll face. If Shirley works from seven in the morning till nine at night, five days a week for seven months solid, she'll still only take home an extra £3,700. She doesn't manage on her wages at the moment, so it's unlikely she'll really be able to save all of that. And even if she does, she'll still have another £1,300 to find to cover the cost of the wedding. Plus the £1,500 she's already got on the credit card. Plus whatever she puts on the new credit card over Christmas. And, of course, she'll barely see Dave at all. Most days, she'll be able to wave to him from the taxi window as he drives one way while she's going the other. Between them, they'll be at the Towers for 120 hours a week. I never hear Shirley complaining, though. Nor anyone else, come to think of it. Most people here seem to be reasonably happy in their work. They've done other jobs where they've been treated much worse and still only earned a similar amount of money. Dave used to be a security guard; Beryl worked in another care home where the routine was much more regimented, where the matron kept a gimlet eye on the staff and never let them so much as sit down, let alone sneak out for a quick fag in the staffroom like they do at the Towers.

Shirley isn't the only one who's worrying about money. It's the time of year for it. Margaret's ten-year-old daughter wants a games computer and a mobile phone for Christmas and she's seriously contemplating whether she can get them for her. Gail and her husband have managed to get a second-hand games computer for *her* nephews and nieces, but even that cost £60. My own calculations have shown you can just about get by on this sort of money around here – but only if you don't have any fun, and you don't run up against any extra expenses. And that you are bound to do, of course. Gail only has a thin jacket to wear, and the temperature is below zero all day long now. The east wind makes it feel even colder than it really is, and her husband's promised to take her into town and treat her to a warm overcoat. She's looked around and picked out the one she wants – a woollen one with fake fur on the collar and cuffs. But when they go into the shop to buy it, she can't bring herself to do it. It's almost £100. She'll find something cheaper, she says. Maybe in the January sales. When winter's half over and she's shivered her way through another month, I think to myself.

The approach of Christmas, as well as Shirley's wedding plans, make me think a lot about the class divide. In some ways, the consumer age has made us less class-ridden in our spending. The income gap between rich and poor may be getting wider, but at least we have equality of aspiration. After all, there can barely be a family in the UK this Christmas, rich or poor, which doesn't have one or more children demanding to be bought the latest PlayStation. It makes a far bigger hole in your budget if you're a care worker than it does if you're on thirty grand a year, of course, but the desire is the same. Mobile phones are just as ubiquitous. So are trainers and designer-label clothes. And I find myself thinking similar thoughts about Shirley's wedding. I know plenty of far wealthier people whose weddings would have been pretty similar to the one she's planning. Naturally, they wouldn't have had to work seventy hours a week for months and months in a vain attempt to pay for theirs. But their plans for their 'big day' would have been pretty similar. I even know one or two couples in London who might well think a stretch limo would be a really cool addition to the special occasion. With a touch of extra irony thrown in just to secure their metropolitan credentials, but at the heart not so different.

And yet, the class structure's still in place. We all know where we are in it. We all know where everyone else is, too. Sally may be nineteen and hoping to become a nurse, but her boyfriend's dad's a doctor. That tells us what we need to know. I'm marked out as middle-class, too. I puzzle over this because it's happened everywhere I've been. What is it about me? I don't have a cut-glass accent. Most of the clothes I'm wearing come from Asda. I've tried to curb my tendency to use long words, though that's harder to disguise. In the end, I decide body language must have a lot to do with it. Maybe it's something we all do. When we think someone is of higher status than us, we don't meet their eye. So if we're looking down as we talk, looking at the person we're talking to but then letting our gaze move quickly away, we're showing respect or submissiveness. I suspect that even when I was dealing with managers, I didn't do this sufficiently. I think I also lacked a certain defensiveness that was often there in my colleagues. I didn't expect to be knocked back, and it showed.

Take Lisa, for example. While Sally isn't afraid to lay herself out for inspection, worrying about whether she performed well enough at her nursing interview, Lisa has a sort of aggression under her cheerful surface that says: 'Don't look at me like that. I can do anything you can, and more.' She's setting out to prove it, mind you. To pay the bills and buy a few 'bits and bobs' for her new flat, she's working not just double shifts but trebles as well. Four days a week she does a fourteen-hour day, from seven in the morning till nine at night. Then on the fifth day she comes in at seven and stays till seven the *next* day. By the time she gets her days off, she's too wrecked to do anything much apart from sleep. When she isn't sleeping, she tends to go round to her mum and dad's to get fed. This does have some advantages, though. Lisa's just had her first electricity bill – £18 for three months, and most of that's service charge. She's hardly had to switch on the cooker or the heating, she says, because she has most of her meals at work and when she gets home she just goes to bed. She's spent £6.50 on gas in the last month. She does occasionally get to go on a night out with her mates, though. I ask her if she ever drinks vodka and Red Bull, and she says she doesn't but she does know where I can find it, if I'm keen. She even gives me directions to a bar in the centre of town that does the Yorkshire thing and sells it by the jug. Bless her. She tells me the drink of choice around these parts is something called a 'blast-off', which she finds hard to describe in detail. Somewhere between aniseed and advocat, she concludes after a few moments' thought.

Some of the staff have to work long hours even if they don't need the money, for the home is constantly under-staffed and always looking for replacements for people who've left. In some ways the problem isn't as acute as it was at Casna or at Bramwells, for many of the staff, once re-cruited, stay for years. But there's clearly a problem getting people to come in the first place. Kitchen staff are a particular problem at the moment. Eddie, the cook, is supposed to have a kitchen porter to help with washing up and preparation, and he's supposed to have someone to relieve him on his days off. But he doesn't, despite a number of ads in the local paper. So he does everything himself. Usually he's in before seven and he leaves about five, after the residents have their tea. Seven days a week. When he tells me he works all week without a break I think he must be having me on. Especially when he adds that Tina's just evil and wants him to suffer, which I think *is* a joke. He's there every day I'm there, even at weekends, so eventually I conclude he's been telling me the truth. An hour or so after we have this conversation, Tina hollers to me from the other side of the hatch between kitchen and dining-room. 'I hear you've been sticking up for him,' she says accusingly, mock-angry. I say oh no, I didn't mean that. I thought he certainly *should* have to work seven days a week, I say. She laughs, but later on I catch her giving me a sharp look.

Ladies, ladies

As the days go by, the residents soon begin to take on individual characters. Lila is a constant presence, not least because she's mobile and tends to wander. At first sight she cuts a rather haughty figure, slightly taller and straighter-standing than most of the residents, and unlike most of them she wears a bra to contain quite an impressive bosom. For many visitors, the sight of her stately progress across the hallway is the first thing they see when they arrive at the Towers. She loves clothes and she often sports a big, flowery blouse and a wide-brimmed straw hat. With her capacious handbag tucked under her arm and her hair carefully permed – there are regular hairdressing sessions – she looks for all the world like a duchess on a day out at the races. Lila has a cheerful air, and as she stands to survey the scene she usually wears a beatific if slightly superior smile. But she has only two words in her regular vocabulary – 'yes', and 'no'. She uses these quite indiscriminately, but despite that it's quite possible to have a lengthy conversation with her.

'Are you well today, Lila?'

'Ye-es.' This is always pronounced with her voice rising at the end of the word, as if she's taken a moment to consider her response and thinks it should be qualified slightly.

'And are you happy?'

'No-oo.'

'Oh dear. Is that because you're hungry? You need your breakfast?'

'No-oo.'

'Is it because you're in the hall and you want to be in the lounge?'

'Ye-es.'

And astonishingly, she allows herself to be led into the lounge, even though I could just as easily elicit the same response by asking if she was missing the magic of the desert skies and the pungent smell of her camel train.

The staff refer to Lila, whose second name is Winston, as 'Winnie'. She doesn't seem to notice, let alone mind. 'Winnie's escaped again!' Lisa will cry as Lila sweeps through the kitchen and out of the back door. Lila merely carries on smiling as she allows herself to be led back indoors. Sometimes, though, I wonder where staff should draw the line. Pat, a female carer who does the breakfasts and organises activities such as bingo for the residents, has taken to whispering words into her ear in the hope that she'll repeat them, which sometimes she does. Pat will lean over significantly with a knowing smile on her face, say something to Lila with a nudge and Lila will respond grandly to the world at large, in Pat's accent rather than her own: 'I'm away to ma bed now wi'a big black man!' Sometimes Lila's mind will play a trick, and fling up some word or phrase which has been lost for years. Sitting at the lunch table, for instance, she may look up with an expression of surprise on her face and remark, quite aptly, 'Cheese sandwiches!' This apparently gives her no more or less pleasure than the rest of her existence, which seems to be reasonably peaceful.

Not all the residents are so unperturbed, though. Poor Ada seems to live in a world of troubles which beset her constantly, keeping her on an endless, restless wandering from which she has to be gently restrained. Take an eye off her for a moment and the next time you look she'll be edging her way across the lounge with her zimmer, as often as not heading for a corner or a narrow point between two chairs where she'll grind to a halt, nudging away gently at the obstacle with her metal frame until someone rescues her. She's frail and shaky, and she's already fallen once and broken her hip so she's not allowed to walk alone. (A similar accident befalls one of the other residents one night when she tries to get out of bed, and I'm amazed at how quickly she's home after her operation. The nurses in the local hospital start her walking after only a couple of days. Sadly, back at the home she's left glowering and miserable in her chair.) Ada is liable to dissolve into genteel tears at the slightest provocation. At first I'm alarmed by this, fearing something is terribly wrong. 'I don't know what to do!' she'll wail, gripped by anguish and with tears pouring down her face. I sit her down, take her hand and ask her what on earth can be the matter. She looks at me, slightly puzzled but still distressed, and repeats: 'I don't know what to do! I'm sure I should be *doing* something!' It's possible to repeat this performance, to reassure her that everything is taken care of, several dozen times within an hour. Get her talking about the shop she used to run, though, or how she once went to London on the train with her husband, and she's fine. She gets regular visitors, but ask her afterwards who they were and she'll shake her head. 'I don't *know*!' she'll quaver, the tears bubbling up once again to the surface. She doesn't know who I am either, of course, but she always seems happy to see me. 'Och darrrling, you'll have to change yourrr teeth! They're afu' sma'!' she will pronounce solemnly, producing one of her rare, kindly smiles as she gazes fondly into my face. But like Lila, Ada is a source of amusement to the staff. 'Right everyone,' Gail will announce, looking around the group of assembled carers. 'Bets on how many minutes it'll be before Ada starts to cry!' And Ada, looking up with a hurt expression on her face and clearly understanding every word, will struggle in vain to contain her tears.

Ada's always conscious of her respectability, holding herself carefully, worrying intensely on the way to the toilet. 'I mustn't pee till I get there! I'm a lady, you know!' she frets one day as we inch our way across the lounge. Others, though, allow old age to free them from their inhibitions. Martha, for instance, looks as if butter wouldn't melt. She has neat white curls framing a sweet if gloomy face whose muscles often seem to be working hard to suppress a smile. But her aggression's never far below the surface. I ask her name on my first day and she replies vehemently: 'A'm Plain

Martha Smith. But I don't know what fucking business it is of yours!' As Gail and Lisa lift her from her wheelchair to put her on the toilet, she cries, 'Get off me you dirty buggers!' But in spite of this, I can't help liking her. There's a humour tucked away below her curmudgeonly surface which is infinitely beguiling. She likes to stay in the dining-room for a fag after lunch, and she has a complicated love life though I never manage to establish for certain whether it's real or imagined. 'How are you today, Martha?' I ask her one day, expecting to be told to mind my own business. 'Not good,' she says, inviting another question. When I ask why, she confides, 'Well, it's all over between Archie and me.'

'Oh dear,' I respond. 'Why is that, then?'

'Ach,' she explains with a sigh. 'Well, he wes nae feckin' use.' Janie, a resident who's a source of useful if not always entirely accurate internal gossip, tells me Archie is Martha's gentleman caller, and that she's heard he's due to come in to see her later on in the day. I don't see him, though.

Martha certainly isn't the only resident who likes to indulge in the odd profanity, and it's a subject which causes some amusement – not to mention bemusement too – among the staff. It comes down to class, Lisa decides one day as we mull the issue over at break. Even if she didn't use those words when she was younger, Martha would certainly have heard them. But the real puzzle is that sometimes when they're really riled, even Ada or Margie will produce words which sound fantastically incongruous. 'Get away from me, you dirty bitch!' Margie shouts at me one night when she's just been given a bath and she's out of sorts. There's nothing in her demeanour that suggests a life spent doing anything more degenerate than the odd day out by the seaside or a rummage around the church jumble sale. It's an odd thought, that those buttoned-up old ladies we see standing at bus stops and in the supermarket are harbouring little caches of filth in the backs of their minds. Who knows when their contents may spring forth, unbidden?

There are some residents who are still quite able to hold on to their personal boundaries, though. There's a little active triumvirate who pass the days knitting, writing letters and doing the crossword puzzles in the *Daily Record*. Janie is the fittest and youngest, at around seventy, and I'm puzzled at first as to why she's here at all. She likes to make herself useful, setting the table for lunch and handing round the biscuits at teatime. But she says she was lonely at home after her husband died, and she likes the company. Emily, a fellow knitter, is much older – nearly ninety – and so is Katie, who seems to be at the centre of a quite phenomenal worldwide web of correspondence. Almost daily, she'll press an airmail letter into someone's hand with instructions to pop it into the post box on the way home. It's often hard to distinguish fact from fiction even with these residents, though. When Katie shows me her Christmas shopping list 'for the troops', I'm inclined to think she's regressed into some sort of wartime fantasy. She's planning to send a couple of dozen small Christmas puddings, biscuits, mince pies, orange juice and two large packets of instant custard. 'They're only a hundred and fifty yards from the border, you know,' she confides knowingly as I smile and nod in mock acquiescence. The next day, I decide to press her further. To exactly which troops is she intending to distribute her largesse? She replies with a detailed description – regiment, battalion, location. They're based in Kosovo at the moment, she explains. She spent a long time in the forces herself, and she likes to keep in touch. They always write her a polite thank-you letter. I feel ashamed for doubting her.

Subordinates

For all its faults the Towers isn't an uncaring place. Some of the staff are virtually saints, doing far, far more than could ever reasonably be expected of them for £4.10 an hour. There's Carol, for example, spending precious minutes making sure Rose is looking smart in a matching blouse and skirt; fussing over whether Lila has had her nails cut or if Ella's had a run-over with the lady-shave and some moisturiser. But there's an edge to relationships between staff and residents which is uncomfortable. It's partly about status, I think. Once you're in an institution, you're a child again. This is partly why Freddie's relationship with Marion is so striking — it reminds us they're adults. Despite being unable to leave this building they still have this small pocket of freedom in which to make decisions for themselves. Freddie still asks Carol to turn her back so he can retain a scrap of privacy while he's changing his underpants, but many of the other residents seem to have given up their control over their bodies, over their personal 'space'. They wouldn't often hug each other, but they expect to get hugged by the staff. With a few exceptions, they submit meekly to having their pants pulled down, their bottoms wiped. They may have been 'Mrs Smith', or 'Mrs Winston', for most of their lives, but now they're 'Plain Martha', or worse, 'Winnie'.

And while they may occasionally lash out verbally or even physically at the staff in moments of frustration, there's not much they can do about their lack of status, their lack of control. I suppose to an extent you'd find this in any nursing home, but it's particularly strong here. There's an atmosphere of cheerful disrespect which per-vades the whole home, and I come to the conclusion that it filters down from Tina. Tina isn't a bad matron. Even though she resents relatives' intrusions she'll call the doctor quite unbidden if she thinks a cut isn't healing properly or a swollen ankle looks dodgy. But the home is her little fiefdom and sometimes I think she treats the residents as her own personal freak-show. 'Winnie!' she'll cry for the benefit of the assembled staff as Lila sails gracefully into the reception area in the morning, beaming over all our heads. 'Winnie! And how are *we* today?' This isn't a question which is likely to get an answer, given Lila's linguistic limitations. Or it'll be Martha, on her way through in her wheelchair with one of the night staff assisting: 'Good *morning*, Martha! Give us one of your lovely smiles, go on!' Martha will glare at her in a 'come-and-have-a-go-if-you-think-you're-hard-enough' kind of way. And Tina will cackle happily. 'Lovely, Martha! So nice to see a cheerful face in the morning!' Sometimes I think the residents are not treated so much a group of disparate and individual adults as a sort of collective joke. There's a great deal of affection in the humour, of course, but it opens the door for something less pleasant. There are 'good' and 'bad' residents. Maud, for example, does nothing but moan and complain. She behaves like a spoilt bairn, and she has to learn not to do that. So when Maud says her colostomy belt's got lost in the wash, no one takes much notice and it doesn't get replaced for months. One day she tells me her ankle is sore – it's been swollen for ages. She has Drapolene on it, she says, so I put some on for her. A couple of days later Maud goes to the hospital for a routine check-up on her arthritis-bound limbs. She comes back in plaster. It seems her ankle's been broken for months and no one's noticed. Tina blames the GP. In the midst of a row about the colostomy belt, Maud blames Tina. I'm unsure. Would the GP really have prescribed Drapolene? Emily is generally regarded as a bloody nuisance, too, running to the toilet every five minutes when she doesn't need to go. Every mealtime, she gets shouted at because she won't eat her dinner. And as for Ada, she drives some of the staff *mad*, fretting and wandering about like that.

It's sweet, frail Ada who's at the centre of the most disturbing incident I witness during my time at the Towers. Usually I work early shifts so I'm not around in the evening, at bathtime. But today I'm on a late and I'm asked to stay in the lounge to keep an eye on the remaining residents while Lisa and a new girl, Louise, take Ada for a bath. I've already been told not to warn the residents it's bath day, as they tend to object. 'Tell them you're going for a walk,' I'm advised. But tonight, with Ada, the pretence is paper-thin. I've seen Lisa pull residents too roughly to their feet before, impatient when they won't stand quickly enough for her. But I've seen nothing like this. 'Ada! Walkies!' she barks, then she instructs Louise to grab Ada under her left arm while she takes the right. Ada's mouth forms into a twisted, pained 'O' as she's yanked to her feet and physically dragged from the room, her legs flailing and failing to make proper contact with the ground. Louise catches my eye. I suspect my own expression mirrors hers, which is one of absolute horror. Ada is crying, but not in her usual, hormonal way. She's terrified, pleading with them, 'Oh, please don't do this to me! Please don't do this to me!' Ten minutes later she's brought back and dumped unceremoniously into her chair. I sit down next to her and she turns to me in a fury. She's not crying now but her forehead is a mottled, angry purple. 'Look what they did to me!' she shouts. 'I'm sorry, Ada …' I say helplessly. And she looks at me with a betrayed expression: 'You could have stood up for me!' You Could Have Stood Up For Me. The words will ring in my ears through a restless night. I know she's right. I could have. And I didn't. Ada goes on, and on. I'm just a twister. I say nice things but really I'm evil and wicked. She's been told all about me. I'm cruel to the poor ones that can't help themselves, and I will get my come-uppance at the gates of heaven for that. She knows my sort. I don't know what to say. What's the point in denying it? After a while she grinds to a halt, and soon I'm called away to help with one of the other residents. Half an hour later Ada is herself again, and she's forgotten all about it. We have a long, rambling conversation about some problem at the post office which is worrying her – some echo of her past life that's impossible for me to fathom. But I can't help feeling depressed by the incident. It makes me feel I'm not cut out for this kind of work. I haven't got the courage to deal with bad situations like that. Afterwards, Louise takes me on one side to confide how upset she was by what happened. She doesn't come in the next day but Ada's still there. And so is Lisa.

Struggling

More than any other minimum-wage job I've done this one needs a huge range of skills, including infinite patience. I suppose part of the problem is at these pay rates, finding staff who have those skills. Surely, I muse, this job could be compared to that of a nursing auxiliary, or even a classroom assistant in a school? Both of those can expect to earn £1,500 a year more than the average newly-recruited care assistant. And both are popularly considered to be criminally underpaid. But the economics of running an institution of this sort in the private sector are dire. One day I pick up the *Nursing Times* in the lounge and it has a long article in it about the crisis in care homes – how lots of them, particularly in this area, are closing because the fees paid by local authorities aren't keeping pace with inflation. The Towers doesn't feel like a place which is rolling in money, with its battered paintwork and its worn carpets. Later, I order up a copy of its annual accounts. The home made a loss running into tens of thousands in the last financial year. The company that owns it lost millions. So, unlike Casna and Bramwells, both of which make healthy profits, the Towers probably can't afford to pay much more than the minimum wage. The vast majority of residents' fees are paid by the local authority so the home's budget is effectively set by the state, even though it's privately owned. Mind you, if we were in the NHS we'd have a union, and there'd be far more effective pressure for better wages, therefore for higher levels of funding. If we were in the NHS, it'd all be so much harder to ignore.

Even despite the low pay, it doesn't surprise me that there are people prepared to do this kind of work. And oddly, one of the reasons for this seems to be connected to the jokey disrespect, the occasional act of downright brutality. For where else can you be paid the minimum wage and still have a higher status than the majority of other people in the place? Where else are the people who effectively pay your wages given so little say in the way you carry out your work? This may seem like a frivolous point, but it isn't. I've found 'unskilled' work bearable, even enjoyable, when there's a sense that someone appreciates my efforts. Without that, the hours grind by in endless tedium or are wasted in paranoid attempts to win acknowledgement that isn't forthcoming. At the Towers, you're largely left alone to get on with the job. Sometimes one of the other staff will grumble if they don't think you're pulling your weight, but there isn't the tense atmosphere which comes of constantly looking over your shoulder. For most of the time, you're in charge. If Ella grumbles for the nineteenth time today that her legs aren't positioned properly in her bed, you can tell her to stop her nonsense if you want. But when Rose looks up at you as you're pulling on her vest and breathes with almost tearful gratitude: 'Oh, I'm so happy to have you doing all this for me …' it's equally OK to let the warmth, the sense of achievement, wash over you.

Living in a box

Caledonian Lodge has its routines, too, but they're more sparse, more spiky than those of the Towers. There are moments of calm followed by short bursts of activity. While the home has a sleepy feel, the lodge is edgy. There's a constant background buzz of pop music, the flavour changing as you move from room to room. The man upstairs from me seems recently to have discovered Pink Floyd's greatest hits and it goes to bed with him, gets up with him. During the week he gets up at five and there's a quick burst of 'Wish You Were Here' or 'Another Brick in the Wall,' then quiet again. At weekends he's never in bed before two. But I don't like to complain. This is partly my English reticence. But it's also a pragmatic decision. The only other CD he seems to own is head-thumping dance music of the five-beats-a-second variety. I fear I may hear more of it if I confess my aversion to his musical heroes. Apart from this irritation, though, life here is comfortable enough. The presence of my fellow-residents is marked mainly by the debris that builds up in the kitchen bin – Scotch pies overlapped by microwave fish and chips, fish and chips trumped by pizza. At around six in the evening there's a series of short, sharp dashes to the microwave. If we time it right, we don't need to coincide at all. I tend to mess up the routine by spending up to half an hour at a time in there, making stews out of cheap cuts of meat I've bought on special offer at Asda. I reckon I can get a main meal for about £1.50 this way. One evening I'm cutting up sprouts and potatoes when a big, bald man of about fifty comes in. He introduces himself as Ted, and tells me he's lived here for five years. He looks curious. After a pause, during which he takes a half-used tin of corned beef from the fridge and squirts some tomato ketchup into it, he plucks up his courage to ask a question. 'Vegetarian, are you?' No, I say, indicating the pot of beef casserole bubbling away on the stove. 'Oh,' he says. 'I just thought you must be, cooking all those vegetables.' Ted is a machine tool operator in a factory, and like many of the people who live here, he works shifts.

Until I came here I had no idea that places like this

existed. Although it's advertised as a hotel it's nothing of the sort. It's a permanent dwelling for most of the residents. But there's nothing cosy, nothing homely about the place. It seems to reduce life to its barest essentials, somehow. It's like a sort of store-cupboard where people go between work and drink, drink and work. I meet one or two other women – one working in town, another a mature student – but they have families, they go home at weekends. The men stay put. There's one young lad who lives in the room opposite mine. He seems to have a job but I never find out what he does. His mum pops round occasionally to make sure he's OK. But Jack and Ted are older, and they're content to stay here long-term. Most of the people are OK, Ted says, but you do get a few weirdos. You know, he says, funny people. When I ask what sort of funny people, he backs off. 'Oh, you know,' he says. 'Pissheads.' I don't actually think this is what he meant. It's already occurred to me that if a caravan park might be an obvious refuge for people evicted from their council houses, Caledonian Lodge would be equally likely to attract people who needed to be anonymous. Sex offenders whose identity's been disclosed to their neighbours, for example? Actually, I feel safer here than I did in either of my previous billets. It's less flimsy than the caravan, less sinister than Strathley Road, with its blocked drains and its boarded-up room. And I don't have to share a bathroom so at least I don't have to venture out into the public areas till

I'm fully clothed. Even more illogically the fact that it's warm and reasonably bug-free makes it feel cosier, more friendly. The lock on the outside door is reassuring, after the wobbly affair I had on the caravan. I know, if I care to think about it, that any danger would be most likely to come from within.

I've busted my budget again, I discover when I do my final sums. My final take-home pay is £400, my total spending £425. That includes the cost of a pair of trousers from Asda and two tunics from the local workwear shop, which I would have had to buy from my first pay cheque if I'd stayed. But, of course, I'd have gone much further into debt if I'd turned up here with no money in the bank. And even though the Towers has paid me correctly for every hour I've worked, my hourly rate is still well below minimum wage once I've deducted the cost of my uniform. Over my first three weeks, it works out at £3.92 an hour.

The Christmas decorations are going up at the Towers as I say my farewells. Carol wishes me luck. Tina says I can come back any time and offers to give me a reference if I should decide to apply for a similar job again. I don't tell most of the residents I'm going. I reckon the majority wouldn't remember who I was by Monday anyway. I tell Ella, though – on one of the few days I didn't get her up she complained about my absence, saying she wanted 'her' carer to wash her. She doesn't really react, just says: 'Oh, well

I'm glad you're getting a break.' After that, I decide not to bother telling Katie or Janie. Although the staff turnover is lower here than in the other places I've worked, there are still enough comings and goings for my departure to pass relatively unremarked. So I just wipe my last bottom, spoon-feed my last lunch, and leave. It's the only place from which I depart with any regrets at all, though. After all, how many jobs are there where you can expect the people you work for to reward you with such unvarnished, heartfelt gratitude and genuine affection?

It's only mid-afternoon when I pull the heavy front door to behind me for the last time but the sky's already beginning to darken and the lights are on indoors. I glance back once as I walk towards the gate. The place looks almost welcoming despite its gloomy outlook and its brooding towers. Lila is standing in an upstairs bay window, surveying the scene. I wave to her, hoping for a response. I can't really see her face, but I hope there's a hint of a smile playing on her lips.

Hours worked: 97.5
Pre-tax pay: £418.40
Take-home pay before uniform   £400.40
Cost of uniforms: £36.00
Hourly pre-tax pay after uniform: £3.92

Spending
Rent and heating: £246.00
Uniform   £36.00
Work trousers: £12.00
Food, etc.:   £131.51
Total spending: £425.51

IV

CONCLUSION

If they say poverty is a great leveller, they are wrong. Poverty doesn't just divide people, it splits them apart like the segments of an orange. From the outside they look like a single, solid mass. Inside they're only aware of their separatenesses, their differences. That's the thing about the nearly poor. That 'nearly' is so important. On £4 an hour or thereabouts you can't afford working-class solidarity. Think about Anna at the Savoy, looking down on the kitchen cleaners and fighting to maintain the sad little pay differential that elevates her above her staff. Think about all the different hats marking out the grades at Bramwells. Status matters, here as much as anywhere.

In general these jobs are boring, they are physically hard and they are alienating. They don't engender bonhomie between the people who do them. That doesn't mean there is never a sense of closeness, but it exists in spite of the conditions, not because of them. Often there is a sense of paranoia. Look at Julie with her bad shoulder, not daring to take a day off sick in case she gets sacked. These people feel the weight of the disrespect coming from above, they feel the flimsiness of the mesh that sits between them and the pit below.

The modern, deregulated labour market is a messy affair, but where the low-paid are concerned it has done a remarkably neat filleting job. Not only are they separated from each other, they are also separated from the rest of society, cut off from many of their most obvious escape routes. Trade unions find it hard to recruit them, not least because they move around a lot or work in places where the unions have never had a strong foothold. In these bottom-of-the-heap jobs there often isn't much career progression, so the chances of moving rapidly up the scale to a better alternative are not great. And where training is on offer, it is more likely to be given to staff who have already have some qualifications or status than it is to people who clean toilets or pack jars into boxes.

There are other aggravating factors which prevent these workers from finding a way of improving their lot. Some are teenagers who've grown up in communities where the culture of work has been lost. They've seen long-term unemployment at close quarters, so it doesn't seem quite so frightening. Many of these will drift in and out of jobs, regarding work as an occasional means of earning some cash rather than as a long-term way of life. They haven't grown up with a sense of pride in where they come from, a sense of what they deserve. If things don't work out, they just move on.

Or maybe, like the Casna staff at the Savoy, they're black, they're in a foreign country and they can only live by working more hours than their student visas allow. Maybe they aren't in any real danger of being deported for breaching their visa conditions, but some of them think they might be. So they carry on working for bad employers, not complaining too loudly when they don't get paid properly because they fear that retribution could follow.

For a variety of reasons the low-paid are left both powerless and voiceless. They feel they have little choice but to put up with being underpaid or being denied their other rights. Because they don't have the leverage to make a difference, they find it easier to walk away from a job than to demand fair play from an employer. And so the carousel swirls on, with workers constantly getting on and off. Few stay in one place long enough to be truly valued, to feel they can speak up and not suffer as a result. And so the next group of recruits comes along and encounters all the same problems as its predecessors.

*

The low-paid have always been at risk of being marginalised, of course. And the Labour Party promised long before it came to power that it would introduce a National Minimum Wage to address the problem. As long ago as 1991 Tony Blair, then Labour's Employment Spokesman, attacked the then Conservative administration for its failure to protect Britain's most vulnerable workers. After all, he argued, was it not Winston Churchill who said in the early years of the twentieth century that the low-paid must be protected to prevent 'the good employer from being undercut by the bad'?

The way forward was the introduction of a minimum wage which could be ratcheted up to end exploitation, Mr Blair said: 'The rest of Europe and the United States not only have a minimum wage but are uprating it by more than inflation. They realise what this Government do not – low wages are not the key to economic success ... Is there not something peculiarly disgusting about those who decry the notion of protection for the lowest paid, yet sit on their hands and do nothing while those in the privatised companies get huge pay rises?'

Those who were instrumental in drawing up Labour's plans for a National Minimum Wage planned that it would be a living wage, enough at least to allow a single person to live a respectable life with decent accommodation and food. Ian McCartney, Tony Blair's successor as Employment Spokesman, told the Commons in 1995 that the reform would allow women, who made up the majority of low-paid workers, to 'take home a living wage'. Just after Labour came to power in 1997 Margaret Beckett, then Trade and Industry Secretary, promised that the new national minimum would 'end the scandal of poverty pay' and would begin to close the growing gap between rich and poor.

All this rhetoric turned out to be somewhat different from the reality that was to follow. The Low Pay Commission, set up by the Labour Government to deliver and monitor the detail of the minimum wage, did not even attempt to discover what income workers would need to be able to live. Apparently one or two of its members did raise the issue of a 'living wage' at an early stage, but their inquiries were quickly squashed. The catchphrase for the exercise, oft-repeated at commission meetings, was 'KISS': Keep It Simple, Stupid. Indeed, the issue of what constitutes a living wage is so complex that virtually nobody has made a serious effort to work out in recent times what it actually means. Instead of trying to calculate what the average single person needs to live, academics, politicians and campaign groups alike tend to skirt the issue. They simply set the so-called 'poverty line' at 50 per cent of the average wage, and adjust their calculations on the numbers in 'poverty' as incomes rise.

The introductory rate for the minimum wage did not even meet this nominal poverty line, though. Set at £3.60, it gave full-time workers take-home pay of around £130 per week, while at the time the 'poverty line' was set at £170 per week. The current rate, of £4.10, gives workers take-home pay of around £140 per week, while the poverty line has risen to around £180. The rate is lower for those aged under twenty-two, having risen from an introductory rate of £3.00 to £3.50 in 2001, and for those under 18 there is no minimum at all. In short, the minimum wage was an old-fashioned political stitch-up, set at a level which would ensure the lowest possible level of protest from employers without enraging the unions sufficiently for them to cause real trouble.

The Low Pay Unit, which runs advice centres, calculated the minimum wage left 3.5 million working families in poverty. Despite this, ministers and the Low Pay Commission alike argued that it had made a difference. The commission calculated in 1999 that it would raise the income of 2 million people who had hitherto been earning even less than the introductory rate. Sadly, its sums were based on incorrect figures published by the Office of National Statistics. The commission has now had to revise its estimate of the number of workers who have benefited downwards to around 1.3 million.

Likewise, other official pronouncements on the subject failed to stand up to close scrutiny. The Chancellor, Gordon Brown, claimed in 2001 that the minimum wage had helped lift 1.2 million children out of poverty. That would be wonderful news, of course, if it were true. In fact, it was based on a mathematical sleight of hand. Treasury officials had calculated that before Labour came to power in 1997, 4.4 million children were living in families whose earnings were less than 50 per cent of the average. If Labour had not been elected, that figure could have gone up to 4.7 million. Instead, between 1997 and 2000 it went down to 3.5 million, a drop of 1.2 million not from the real level but from a theoretical, projected level. Furthermore, a glance back at some of Mr Brown's pre-1997 pronouncements reveals that at the time he calculated 4.2 million children, not 4.4 million, were in poverty. If this was correct, the real number whose lives improved was not 1.2 million but 700,000, with the number falling from 4.2 million to 3.5 million.

This is still significant, of course. But was the minimum wage responsible? Most families in poverty live not on low wages but on benefits. And between May 1997 and December 2001, the number of people claiming unemployment benefit fell from 1.6 million to 960,000. In January 2002, a record 28.2 million people were in work. So, many of those 700,000 children rose above the poverty line not because their parents started taking home the minimum wage, but because they signed off unemployment benefit and started working.

There were also claims that the minimum wage had helped to close the gap between the top and bottom of the pay scale. In 1999, the year the minimum wage was introduced, the wages of the bottom 10 per cent of workers rose faster than those of the top 10 per cent, according to a report from the Low Pay Commission. This, too, was based on inaccurate figures in the Government's annual New Earnings Survey. They had been skewed by the omission of a few of the highest-paid workers from the statistical sample on which the survey was based. The gulf between rich and poor, growing ever wider over the past two decades, had not started to shrink at all. It later became clear that the gap between the bottom 10 per cent of full-time workers and the top 10 per cent did not narrow when the minimum wage was introduced. In the first year it stayed roughly the same, with the lowest-paid earning a little more than a quarter of the pay of the highest, and in the second year it widened slightly.

There is another major factor in raising families out of poverty: top-up benefits, paid to working parents to ensure that even if their wages are low, their children's basic needs are met. One of the key arguments for the introduction of a minimum wage was that these benefits were costing the state a fortune – £2.4 billion in the last year before the reform. Even after the 1997 election, ministers condemned the 'poverty pay' that made such top-ups necessary. In December 1997, Margaret Beckett described the benefits as 'a massive cost to the public purse' and blamed the low-wage economy which had developed under successive Tory governments: 'The taxpayer is paying a heavy price for the previous Government's decision to remove any floor on earnings,' she said. So did the minimum wage lift earnings to such a degree that it cut the cost of top-up benefits? Not at all. In fact the bill for such benefits, fuelled by the introduction of a new and more generous system, more than doubled to £5.2 billion between 1999 and 2001. So under the new minimum wage, the Government achieved the complete opposite of what it said it had set out to do. It might, of course, be possible to argue that despite the Government's protestations these top-up benefits are a perfectly good way of ensuring that people who go to work have enough to live on. However, this is not the case because a third of the people who are entitled to the benefits do not claim them.

What really matters, of course, is whether people actually feel better off. When the official 'poverty line' is simply a percentage of the average income, it stands to reason that a proportion of the population are always going to be below it. So how does it *feel* to take home the minimum wage? Here the official statistics have less to tell us. The Low Pay Commission consults stakeholders before it publishes its reports on whether the minimum wage is working. But the list seems remarkably thin on representatives of the low-paid. The commission talks to the Confederation of British

Industry, the Federation of Small Businesses and a host of associations representing industries such as hospitality, hairdressing, textiles. It also talks to the Trades Unions, but most of their members earn more than the minimum wage.

The commission does pay for a small quantity of what is sometimes rather sneeringly referred to as 'touchy-feely research'. This is carried out by the few organisations which are in touch with the low-paid – the Low Pay Unit, Citizens' Advice Bureaux and community groups. In one such piece of work, the Low Pay Unit followed the fortunes of forty-five workers who asked its advisers for information about the minimum wage before its introduction. Its report made illuminating reading. For while most of the workers were paid the minimum, their employers found many and ingenious ways of taking back the money. Before the introduction of the minimum wage, these workers were earning between £1.50 and £3.50 an hour. Three of them found they were not eligible for the minimum, two because they were under eighteen and one because the sleepovers she did in a nursing home for £1.58 an hour were not counted as 'work'. Five months after the introduction of the legal minimum, six eligible workers were still working for less. Five had received the minimum, but only belatedly. Two had been sacked because their employers did not want to pay them the minimum. Ten had received pay rises but had suffered at the same time from cuts in hours, the withdrawal of paid rest breaks, cuts in overtime pay or in bonuses. The workers who talked to the Low Pay Unit were the stroppy ones. They were prepared to go out and find out what their legal rights were. And even then, some of them decided not to pursue the issue for fear of retribution. How many more voiceless employees were there who simply carried on regardless, perhaps aware of their rights, perhaps not, but feeling powerless to do anything about them?

*

There are simple things that could be done to give the nearly poor a voice. Trade unions could try harder to recruit them. Companies could be ordered to put big notices on the walls of the offices where they hand out the pay slips, explaining just what they should be paying and what they shouldn't be deducting. Advertisements could be placed on public transport, bearing the phone numbers of Low Pay Units and Citizens' Advice Bureaux. The Low Pay Commission could follow the fortunes of a sample of low-paid workers, to pick up on the ways their rights are undermined by their employers.

But such things would just be tinkerings. The low-paid need a voice at the heart of Government. When the notion of a Low Pay Commission was first mooted it was suggested it should play that role – that it should be able to stand up and shout about the sufferings of the most vulnerable workers, and that when it did so the Government would be forced to listen. But instead it ended up as a coalition, none of whose members held a torch for those at the bottom of the heap. The commission consists of three academics, three trade unionists and three employers' representatives. Its aim is to produce a compromise view, to speak with one voice, and so that voice can only ever be a muted, measured one. Employers, of course, have to have their interests balanced against those of their workers. The academics can have their say, but they have to try to steer a neutral course. Even the trade unionists have their members to think of, and though they advocate a higher minimum they have to wonder whether big rises for the lowest-paid would encroach on the next people up the scale. All have to consider the conventional economic view that a too-high minimum wage can lead to rises in unemployment, though there has been little evidence of this happening so far in the UK. So who can speak unambiguously on behalf of the low-paid, on the body that's supposed to tell the Government their woes? No one. And that should change.

Members of the Low Pay Commission would say, quite correctly, that they do not have a remit to speak up for the low-paid. Look at their terms of reference, set out for them by the Government, and this becomes clear. The commission is not currently charged with finding out whether or not employers are paying the minimum wage. Instead, they have been asked to look at the effect of the minimum on employment and competitiveness, on pay differentials and on the tax and benefit systems.

The commission did say, in its third report, that things seemed to be working well. Most employers were paying the minimum wage. But if my experience was anything to go by, that sweeping statement could mask a much more disturbing reality. All the employers I worked for were paying the minimum wage, or they would have said they were if anyone had asked. In fact, over the total 356 hours I worked, I received an average of £3.80 an hour before tax but after illegal deductions. And all the jobs I did were supposed to pay more than the minimum. In my first job I was supposed to be paid £4 an hour when the minimum was £3.70, but actually I got £3.43. In the second, by which time the minimum was £4.10, I was supposed to get minimum wage plus extra for turning up regularly and a premium for overtime, but actually I got £3.89. In the third, I was supposed to get £4.20 plus extra at the weekend, but I got £3.92.

This sleight of hand was achieved by my employers in a variety of ways. Two of them 'lost' hours when they were doing the wages. One of them made employees work an unpaid 'training day', and also imposed administrative charges for paying their wages into the bank. All of them made their employees pay for the protective clothing they were legally required to provide. In addition to these things, two of my employers seemed to be failing in their duties to pay sick pay. Two of them made their employees work several months before giving them their entitlement to paid holidays. They were able to cut their bills in legal ways, too. None paid for breaks – employees must have breaks, but employers do not have to pay for them. Two of my employers made me wait a month before I got paid.

But even if the Low Pay Commission were asked to look at issues such as these, would it have muscle to do anything about it? Would it, as one of the architects of the reform put it when I spoke to him, have a big stick? Of course, it would never be possible completely to stamp out the ruses used by employers to keep wage bills down. But vigorous and thorough enforcement could help. At the moment, employers are meant to be kept in line by a network of inspection teams run by the Inland Revenue. In the first two years of the minimum wage the revenue investigated 6,400 complaints. It found 3,200 employers who were not complying, but it only issued 349 enforcement notices and sixty-two penalty notices. There were no prosecutions. Furthermore, the inspectors only targeted those employers who were thought most likely to be blatantly flouting the law. Those who fiddled in the margins, as my employers did, were unlikely ever to be visited, let alone picked up.

So we see the bird swimming on the surface – the high-profile cases which make the papers, for example the group of Indian stonemasons building a temple in London who were found to be earning Indian wages of thirty pence an hour and were awarded £100,000 in back-pay – and we assume there is plenty of vigorous paddling going on under the water-line. In fact, there isn't much else happening at all.

The worst employers are more likely to be picked up not because they're failing to pay minimum wage but because they're using illegal immigrants or benefit claimants. During my time in Yorkshire I nearly had a brush with this sort of enforcement action myself. I'd made contact with a middle-aged woman called Annie who'd been working for one of these employers. Lots of women do, in the poorer parts of the North. They get picked up at four in the morning by a minibus which takes them to where there's casual labour available that day. After paying their bus fares they're dropped off again in the late afternoon with £20 in their hands – if they've worked a full day. Some days they only work a few hours, and that's all they get paid for. Their bus fare is still taken out of the pot first, of course. They might end up cutting flowers in Lincolnshire, or packing sandwiches in the Midlands. Annie was going to put me in touch with the gang leader who organised the labour so I could try to get on the bus myself. But the week I arrived in town, they were raided in a factory in Barnsley. Most were claiming benefit, of course. The next week it was reported there'd been a similar incident in York, in which a double-decker bus carrying foreign workers was stopped on its way to a workplace in the city. Annie told me her local minibuses were off the road, waiting for quieter times. I don't know about the Barnsley incident, but the press report from York suggested the raid there was carried out by benefits and immigration officials, not Inland Revenue inspectors. But the truth is Annie's employers were guilty not just of using illegal labour, but also of failing to pay the minimum wage. She told me those workers had to be really desperate to agree to do what they did. They certainly weren't in a position to phone the Inland Revenue to complain that they weren't getting the minimum wage.

If minimum wage enforcement teams were linked to the Low Pay Commission, the role of the commission would change beyond recognition. Instead of acting as an amalgam of all the interested parties except the low-paid themselves, it would have a direct line to those people who are hardest hit when it doesn't work – or rather, those people would have a direct line to it. Then, instead of simply reporting- as it did last year – that many people thought the Inland Revenue inspectors should be more pro-active, it could actually do something about it.

*

That watchword – Keep It Simple, Stupid – was a perfectly serviceable one when the imperative was to deliver a minimum wage with minimum fuss. Too much complicated debate about how much people really needed to live on and the whole exercise could have collapsed in acrimony at an early stage amid claim and counter-claim. Too much detail, with different rates for different areas, and the employers could have dismissed the whole scheme as unworkable. Over the whole exercise hung the spectre of the old Wages Councils, abolished by the Conservatives, and the complex negotiations which used to go on about how much should be paid in each sector, each region. No one wanted to revisit that 1970s labour relations scenario.

The result, though, has been a minimum wage which has only partially achieved its aims. In the more expensive areas of the country, as my experience made clear, it simply does not work. After all, how could it? A single national minimum wage could never be effective because we do not have a single national cost of living. If the minimum was set at a level on which people could live in London, it would put thousands out of work in Belfast. Set, as in my opinion it has been, at a rate which is just about adequate for the cheapest areas, it has little or no effect on poverty in the South East or in the more expensive parts of the rest of the United Kingdom.

The bottom line about the minimum wage is that it is simply too low. It is not a solution to the problems of Britain's poorest workers. One of the most shocking things I heard while talking to some of the major players about this issue was the justification that it was all right to have a very low minimum wage because three quarters of people earning it were women. By virtue of their sex they were, according to this argument, not the main breadwinners for their families. It is all right not to pay people a living wage *because they are women*. For the record, the vast majority of the women I met were not 'second wage earners' at all. Some of them were bringing up their children alone, others lived in shared houses with large numbers of other adults. Some of them had husbands or partners in minimum-wage jobs. Some of them had husbands or partners who did not work at all. A few had partners with better-paid jobs, of course. But most of them would not have been getting up at five o'clock in the morning to stack bottles, or getting on the tube at midnight to go and scrub urinals, if their husbands had been earning a living wage. For most of those women, whether they worked full-time or part-time, the money they took home formed a major part, if not *the* major part of their family's budget.

Another false assumption I encountered was the idea that imposing a minimum wage for under-eighteens would simply lead to higher levels of youth unemployment, and that this would be unequivocally a bad thing. This is a tricky issue, of course – no one would want to suggest that school leavers would be better off on the streets than in work. But I would question the value of recruiting large numbers of teenagers into dead-end agency jobs at an age when they are best placed to enrol in the local college and learn a skill. In the Yorkshire factory where I worked there were large numbers of youngsters packing pickles. As most of them would not have been entitled to benefits, they had a straight choice between staying in education and looking for work. Ken at Temps R Us told me he was always trying to keep a balance between older workers, who were more reliable, and younger ones who – though he didn't spell this out – were cheaper. If employers like Bramwells saw no financial advantage in employing these young people as casual labour, they would not do it. And some of those young people might stay in education instead.

At its heart the minimum wage is a political stitch-up, designed to deliver a manifesto pledge demanded by old Labour and the unions. The key, hinted at as long ago as 1991 by Tony Blair, was to put it in place without causing any discomfort to the employers. This had its virtues, of course. The minimum wage would not have helped anyone if it had never got off the ground in the first place. But now we have managed to implement the reform without pain, it is time to move on from there. This measure was meant to make a difference to people's lives. Otherwise, what was it for? The difference made, so far as I could see, was minimal. Not once during my period of low-paid work did I hear any of my workmates say things had got better for them as a result of the minimum wage.

The minimum wage was a much-needed reform that stalled while ministers sat mesmerised and frozen like rabbits in the headlights of the employers' juggernaut. And every day the Government fails to act, Anna endures her hour-and-a-half bus journey to the Savoy. Every day, Dave and Duncan get up at 4.30am to catch the Bramwells minibus. Every day Shirley works her fourteen hours, hoping against hope she'll be out of debt before her wedding day.

ACKNOWLEDGEMENTS

Thanks are due to Ian Katz of the *Guardian* for the idea which led to this book being written, and to Andrew Franklin at Profile Books for commissioning it. Also to Sarah Wilson, Peter Gannon, Judith Thompson, Angie Ruane, Sue Clark, Lynda Milner, Angie Beardsley, Andy Sidney, Karen and Tom, Isobel Howie and Owen McDowell, all of whom gave support and advice. And, of course, to my partner Phil Solomon, who gave more than anyone. I am grateful to Catherine Capon and Kate Harre at the Low Pay Commission and to Professor William Brown, one of the low pay commissioners, for his comments. Also to Jeff Masters at the Low Pay Unit and to Fred Bayliss, whose historical perspective and current-day insight were invaluable. The idea sprang from Barbara Ehrenreich's book, *Nickel and Dimed*.